At Issue

Medical Malpractice

Other Books in the At Issue Series:

At Issue

I Medical Malpractice

Noah Berlatsky, Book Editor

GREENHAVEN PRESS

A part of Gale, Cengage Learning

GALE
CENGAGE Learning·

Farmington Hills, Mich • San Francisco • New York • Waterville, Maine
Meriden, Conn • Mason, Ohio • Chicago

Patricia Coryell, *Vice President & Publisher, New Products & GVRL*
Douglas Dentino, *Manager, New Products*
Judy Galens, *Acquisitions Editor*

For more information, contact:
Greenhaven Press
27500 Drake Rd.
Farmington Hills, MI 48331-3535
Or you can visit our Internet site at gale.cengage.com

Articles in Greenhaven Press anthologies are often edited for length to meet page requirements. In addition, original titles of these works are changed to clearly present the main thesis and to explicitly indicate the author's opinion. Every effort is made to ensure that Greenhaven Press accurately reflects the original intent of the authors. Every effort has been made to trace the owners of copyrighted material.

Cover image © Images.com/Corbis.

LIBRARY OF CONGRESS CATALOGING-IN-PUBLICATION DATA

Medical malpractice / Noah Berlatsky, book editor.
     pages cm. -- (At issue)
     Summary: "At Issue: Medical Malpractice: Books in this anthology series focus a wide range of viewpoints onto a single controversial issue, providing in-depth discussions by leading advocates, a quick grounding in the issues, and a challenge to critical thinking skills"-- Provided by publisher.
     Includes bibliographical references and index.
     ISBN 978-0-7377-7175-6 (hardback) -- ISBN 978-0-7377-7176-3 (paperback)
     1. Physicians--Malpractice--United States. 2. Tort liability of hospitals--United States. 3. Medical personnel--Malpractice--United States. I. Berlatsky, Noah.
     KF2905.3.M4377 2014
     344.7304'11--dc23

                                                                    2014030220

Printed in the United States of America
1 2 3 4 5 6 7 18 17 16 15 14

Contents

Introduction

This book largely focuses on medical malpractice laws, issues, and controversies in the United States. However, other countries also struggle with issues surrounding medical malpractice. Like the United States, they too try to balance the need to protect patients from medical error with the need to protect providers from frivolous lawsuits. One country with a very different system, but similar concerns, is the United Kingdom (UK).

In contrast to the United States, where health insurance is provided by private businesses, the United Kingdom has a single-payer health system. This means that the government is the provider of all insurance to all UK citizens. Thus, "the National Health Service (NHS) employs most physicians and administers all of the legal and business aspects of practicing medicine,"[1] according to Thomas B. Fleeter, writing for the American Academy of Orthopaedic Surgeons.

Since the NHS is the centralized provider of health care in the United Kingdom, physicians are not personally liable for negligence. Instead, if there is a medical error, the NHS is considered to be the responsible party. Patients effectively sue the government. Payments come out of government budgets, and are ultimately funded by taxpayers.

After it is sued, the NHS decides whether to fight each claim or whether to settle. The UK government works to avoid litigation; only a small number of claims go to trial, and most of these are resolved in a year and a half. In a report for the Law Library of the US Library of Congress, Clare Feikert states that in 2007–2008, the NHS reported that 41 percent of claims were abandoned by the claimant, 41 percent were settled out of court, and 4 percent went to trial, though most

---

1. Thomas B. Fleeter, "Worldwide Trends in Medical Liability," *AAOS Now*, September 2011. www.aaos.org/news/aaosnow/sep11/managing4.asp.

of these were actually court approvals of negotiated settlements rather than actual trials. A final 14 percent remained outstanding at the end of the year.[2]

So far this sounds like an improvement on the US health system, especially to the extent that UK doctors are not frightened of lawsuits and therefore have no incentive to practice defensive medicine by scheduling extra tests in order to protect themselves. In practice, however, the UK system is far from perfect. In fact, many of the complaints about the system are similar to complaints in the United States. Feikert notes, for example, that there are concerns that the system for redress is too complicated, too slow, and too costly, and that its inefficiencies damage public faith in the NHS. Patients are also dissatisfied, Feikert writes, "with the lack of explanations and apologies or reassurances that action has been taken to prevent the same incident happening to another patient."[3] This again parallels concerns in the United States, where fear of lawsuits can keep hospitals from disclosing records and prevent doctors from talking openly to patients. Along those lines, Feikert says, there is concern that the fear of payouts causes the NHS to be secretive and defensive, which obstructs health-care improvements.

In an April 2012 article in the *Chicago-Kent Law Review,* Richard Goldberg argues that problems with medical lawsuits have been intensified in recent years by the financial crisis and subsequent government austerity measures in the United Kingdom. The government has been especially worried because the numbers of claims and payouts have been rising over the last few years. The government blames this increase on the proliferation of no-win no-fee attorneys. These lawyers take cases and agree to be paid only if there is a settlement, putting their services within reach of many more claimants. Generally, suc-

2. Clare Feikert, "Medical Malpractice Liability: United Kingdom (England and Wales)," Library of Congress, May 2009. www.loc.gov/law/help/medical-malpractice-liability /uk.php.
3. Ibid.

cessful lawyers have their fees paid by the defendants in the case (in this case, the NHS). Legislation has been proposed in the United Kingdom to reduce these kinds of lawsuits by requiring payment to come from the successful claimant. Since the fee would come out of the settlement, it would reduce the amount a client would win, and so reduce the incentive to sue.

Goldberg, however, argues that the NHS's fears about rising lawsuits appear to be overblown (much as in the United States, where many doctors overestimate the likelihood of a malpractice suit). "[I]t is premature to suggest that such an increase in claim numbers during the last two years should give rise to the degree of concern that appears to have emanated" from the government, he argues, adding that the growth of no-win no-fee lawyers has been a boon for patients. "[I]t is clear," he says, "that there has been a marked increase in access to justice over the last ten years in this area and this is to be welcomed."[4] Along these lines, Goldberg opposes the UK government's plan to eliminate legal aid for negligence claims, arguing that this may prevent patients who have been the victims of medical error from obtaining compensation.

The authors of the viewpoints in *At Issue: Medical Malpractice* touch on many of the issues surrounding medical malpractice confronted by the United Kingdom, as well as other concerns unique to the United States, such as the pros and cons of malpractice caps, the value of so-called safe-harbor laws, the use of health courts, and the potential impact of the Patient Protection and Affordable Care Act, popularly known as the ACA or "Obamacare," on medical practice in the country.

4. Richard Goldberg, "Medical Malpractice and Compensation in the UK," *Chicago-Kent Law Review*, vol. 87, no. 1, 2012, pp. 131–61. http://scholarship.kentlaw.iit.edu /cklawreview/vol87/iss1/7.

Physicians Have a Justified Fear of Malpractice Lawsuits

Evan Levine

Evan Levine is a cardiologist and the author of What Your Doctor Won't (Or Can't) Tell You.

Doctors work under a real and justified fear of frivolous and malicious lawsuits. Patients fail to realize that no doctor can prevent bad outcomes 100 percent of the time, while unscrupulous lawyers look to profit from big money lawsuits. Lawsuits are not only expensive but they distract doctors and reduce the time they can spend with their patients. The primary concern in such malpractice cases does not seem to be the welfare of the patient but rather the opportunity for a payout.

While I believe that medical malpractice is endemic in the United States, I urge readers also to understand the burden under which every doctor has to practice. This burden can be expressed as a simple question: Can anyone be expected to be right 100% of the time?

Practicing in Fear

All physicians practice with the fear that one day we may be sued, and sued for more than their malpractice insurance covers. Would anyone wish to work under these conditions? What most people don't realize is that poor outcomes do not necessarily mean malpractice. All procedures have risks. All medications have risks. Yet, some malpractice attorneys, in carefully thought out business decisions, seek out cases with huge potential pay-offs even if no malpractice is involved. They then try to spin these cases to make it seem that there was malpractice involved because if they convince the jury, there is a huge payday awaiting them.

I was sued over a case once and I will never forget it. The case dragged on for years which meant that I had to reveal in every reappointment to every hospital and insurance plan that I had been named in a lawsuit. I was told by my attorneys that I needed to ready for the case; that it might go to court at any time (even as I was preparing for my honeymoon) and that I would have to arrange my schedule to ensure that I was available. As a matter of policy, my insurance company told me that I should be in court every day, even if the case dragged on for weeks, and even if it meant I would not be able to see my patients; they do this because they feel that the jury will perceive the defendant as uncaring if he does not show up each day.

It seemed to me that none of the lawyers, either the malpractice attorney or my defense team, seemed to care about the patient or the doctor. What most of the businessmen involved seemed really to care about was the money.

The case dragged on for years, possibly because the malpractice attorney did not have a case, and could not find a credible expert witness.

What was really hurtful was the fact that I was even sued. The patient had first seen another cardiologist who had missed the fact that she had suffered a heart attack. She only learned of the heart attack after coming to see me for an opinion. I repeated an echocardiogram, at no cost to her, and told her that the previous doctor had incorrectly read her study—and that while he had said that she had not had a heart attack, it was quite clear to me that she had. I placed her on medications that possibly saved her life and sent her for a coronary angiogram.

During this angiogram the patient suffered a stroke that resulted, in what she claimed, was some type of periodic visual disturbance. The doctor who performed the angiogram was sued as well, though the complication was not an uncommon one. Much of the suit, however, centered on why I had sent the patient for the angiogram. Again, no party ever expressed concern about the doctor who got the diagnosis wrong—the angiogram confirmed everything I said—even though he had clearly missed identifying the MI [myocardial infarction, or heart attack] in this patient.

The Case Drags On

The case dragged on for years, possibly because the malpractice attorney did not have a case, and could not find a credible expert witness. But the case seemed to center on two things.

1. The patient admitted that she was told she could die from the test, but not that she might suffer a stroke.

2. That I acted inappropriately in ordering a coronary angiogram and not a nuclear stress test. I believe the plaintiff's attorney also tried to insinuate that I asked for the angiogram because coronary angiograms pay more.

The truth is is that the patient signed not one but two informed consents with the possibility of stroke mentioned on each of them—the duplication occurred because her initial date was canceled after she arrived to the hospital with flu-like symptoms, and after she reviewed and signed the consent. She returned a week later and repeated the process.

The angiogram was done not because of any financial reward (I am actually paid over two times as much by insurers to perform a nuclear stress test vs. an angiogram) but because it is the procedure recommended in the guidelines published by the American College of Cardiology.

As the years went by I was asked over and over again to review the case with my attorney, who felt I was not part of the team because I was reluctant to waste another day dealing with this dreadful case instead of caring for my patients. I remember telling him, "You tell me I am not a team player. I guess I cannot be part of the team when you are earning thousands of dollars for this case, getting paid for every minute you spend with me, and asking me to neglect my patients and come visit you to review your case. When I get paid, like you do, then perhaps I will be more motivated to be part of your team."

In the end, perhaps seeing that his case was going nowhere, the plaintiff's lawyer asked the hospital to offer him a settlement. On the condition that he agreed that none of the doctors were at fault, the plaintiff's attorney accepted an offer of $25,000: about $8,000 for him for his ten years of work, and the rest to the plaintiff and her family.

2

Malpractice Fears Obscure a Crisis in Medical Ethics

John Lynch

John Lynch founded and served as chairman, president, and chief executive officer of Medical Diagnostics, Inc., a company that produces and markets a network of mobile MRI (magnetic resonance imaging) clinics.

Malpractice fears tend to be overblown and do not get at the root of the real problems in health care. Some physicians use fears of a medical malpractice lawsuit as an excuse to prescribe costly tests. Others use it as an excuse to keep information about tests and care from patients in violation of medical ethics. Reform should focus on bringing greater transparency to medical procedures and in providing medical consumers with more information about the services they receive.

Medical malpractice in America remains a thorny and contentious issue, made no less so by its virtual exclusion from the Affordable Care Act (ACA, or Obamacare) [officially the Patient Protection and Affordable Care Act] governing healthcare reform in America.

Missing from Obamacare

Which is why I was glad to see the former head of President [Barack] Obama's Office of Management and Budget, Peter Orszag, now with the liberal Center for American Progress, cite it as his second top priority for gaining control of our out-sized medical spending—an implicit criticism of its omission from Obamacare.

Although speaking in the context of criticizing Rep. Paul Ryan's (R-WI) plan to offer vouchers so Medicare enrollees could purchase private health insurance, his comments about the need to address malpractice reform are a departure from the liberal talking points on Obamacare. Here's what he had to say. . . .

"If I had to pick out two or three things to do immediately, I would pick the accelerated (trend) towards bundled payments and non fee-for-service payment. . . .

"The second thing, which might be a little more controversial, both substantively and politically, is to *put forward a more aggressive medical malpractice reform.* . . .

"When I go out and talk to heath care groups, if you start out with the fact that you acknowledge that whatever the academic literature says, that it would be beneficial if we could provide more clarity to doctors, the conversation changes. And I think it would be beneficial for supporters of the Affordable Care Act (Obamacare) to change the conversation in that way," Orszag claimed (emphasis added).

The malpractice threat is often just an excuse to keep practicing in ways that drive up medical spending because it's highly profitable to do so.

It's too bad Obamacare doesn't include more substantive approaches to tackling the malpractice issue. The actual potential for cost-savings from malpractice reform as it's generally considered is slim. Not a single state that's adopted some form of malpractice reform has shown any savings from it.

But Orszag's point is that addressing the issue substantively in Obamacare would have helped to defuse it as an excuse for the rampant overdiagnosis and treatment going on in American healthcare. I cite one survey in [his book] *Our Healthcare Sucks* in which 94% of surveyed physicians admitted to practicing so-called "defensive medicine" designed primarily to protect themselves from perceived risk of malpractice lawsuits.

I also do a crude analysis suggesting the rate of needless hospitalizations admitted to in that survey—which was one in eight hospitalizations—was roughly a 100-to-1 overreaction to the actual risk of malpractice lawsuits. If nothing else, making some substantive changes to current malpractice laws might help to temper such overreactions—although the experience in Texas and other states that have passed malpractice reform legislation in the still-dominant fee-for-service payment system found no change in medical practices that remain highly lucrative.

In other words, the malpractice threat is often just an excuse to keep practicing in ways that drive up medical spending because it's highly profitable to do so. Malpractice risk provides a convenient cover for many doctors, though not all. There are certain specialties that remain hard hit by malpractice premiums that would benefit from sensible reforms to existing laws—whether in Obamacare or otherwise.

The "Mal" in Malpractice

Malpractice reform—whether in the context of Obamacare or more broadly—is always framed as a problem for physicians. They're victims of overzealous lawyers and an overly litigious society. But are they really the victims here?

Here's a quote from *Our Healthcare Sucks* taken from a study in a major medical journal:

> Medical errors are common, frequently result in considerable human morbidity and mortality, and often are avoidable. . . . Threats of legal liability are more compelling than altruistic motives. . . .

The *American College of Physicians Ethics Manual* states that a physician is obliged to disclose "information (to patients) about procedural or judgment errors made in the course of care if such information is material to the patient's well-being." . . .

Reporting medical errors represents a conflict of interest for physicians . . . (that's led to) a veil of secrecy that surrounds medical errors.

According to a report in *Forbes* magazine: "One in 200 patients who spend a night in a (U.S.) hospital will die from medical error."

Malpractice claims are at record lows despite persistent medical errors.

An entire chapter in *Our Healthcare Sucks* is devoted to the subject of medical errors. Among other things, it notes that malpractice claims are at record lows despite persistent medical errors that account for well in excess of 100,000 deaths annually in America.

And medical errors remain a much bigger problem in America than in other developed countries. . . .

The true and lasting solution to our medical malpractice problem requires much more than caps on damages that limit financial liability—a formula that's proven to do nothing to lower medical costs in the states in which it's been enacted. A more realistic solution is described in Part 3 of [Lynch's book] *Obamacare—The Good, the Bad & the Missing*, summarized briefly as follows. . . .

Malpractice Reform + Medical Error Reporting + Stronger Informed Consent

The following is excerpted from the book:

In states that have capped damages for patients' pain and suffering, medical overtreatment has continued long after the malpractice insurance concern has been relieved. This means no savings are realized by medical consumers despite sacrificing legal rights. . . .

But comprehensive reform needn't come off the backs of patients. True malpractice reform requires more than capping damages for victims of malpractice. This simplistic but superficial approach—like American medicine itself—addresses only symptoms while ignoring the underlying causes. . . .

Capping patient damages has consistently failed to reduce malpractice premiums or consumers' health insurance bills in states in which it's been tried. What's needed instead is comprehensive reform targeting medical errors and other causes of malpractice claims. . . .

To implement malpractice reform without requiring greater transparency in public reporting of medical errors—which is currently inhibited by malpractice liability—would fail to capture one of the main reasons to undertake malpractice reform. . . .

The third leg of this three-legged approach to malpractice reform would include a strengthened program of 'Informed Consent' as part of a broader patient education initiative designed to make patients better medical consumers. This is the most promising approach to not only malpractice reform, but to smarter use of our expensive medical system.

This kind of comprehensive approach to malpractice reform that targets not the superficial consequences of malpractice—patient damages—but its root *causes* is sorely among "The Missing" in Obamacare. And its free-market alternative would deregulate healthcare reform and very likely exacerbate medical errors and the malpractice claims they will generate.

"A Conspiracy of Silence"

An article in the *Journal of Patient Safety* that's cited in *Our Healthcare Sucks* had this to say about this subject:

When it is clear that our care has caused preventable harm and we allow a conspiracy of silence to betray those who have put their faith in us, we inflict the impact and pain that is *nothing short of a "hit and run" accident* (emphasis added).

As but one example, the book cites a survey finding that 6 out of 7 radiologists were unwilling to admit mammogram screening errors to patients. That makes this accepted medical practice even though it explicitly violates the AMA's [American Medical Association] Code of Ethics.

This is the true crisis in American healthcare—the crisis of deteriorating medical ethics that's behind much of our actual medical malpractice and our unnecessary spending to fatten the wallets of unscrupulous doctors and hospitals.

Malpractice reform is just a smoke screen that distracts from the all too real injury, including death, that's inflicted on unsuspecting patients and their families each and every day in America—Obamacare or no Obamacare.

3

Malpractice Caps Ensure Good Care for Patients

Nathanial Nolan

Nathanial Nolan is a student at the University of Missouri-Columbia School of Medicine. His writing on health-care quality and medical education has appeared in the Columbia Daily Tribune, Missouri Medicine, *and on KevinMD.com.*

Removing medical malpractice damage caps increases frivolous lawsuits without reducing medical malpractice. Missouri removed caps during the early 2000s and the result was a spike in lawsuits, the overwhelming majority of which were frivolous and resulted in no conviction. In addition, doctors began to leave the state after the caps were removed. A new cap was instituted in 2005, stemming the rush of lawsuits, but in 2012 the Missouri Supreme Court ruled that the caps were unconstitutional and overturned the 2005 law that restored them. Since history shows, however, that removing caps drives doctors out of the state and does not help patients, a cap on damages should be reinstituted.

A decade ago, Missouri medicine was in crisis mode after the revocation of the state malpractice cap. In the mid-1980s, Missouri set laws that limited noneconomic damages in medical malpractice cases at $350,000—a limit that was indexed based on inflation and thus would increase annually. In 2002, the Missouri Eastern District Court of Appeals issued a decision in *Scott v. SSM Health Care* that effectively nullified the cap. As part of the decision, the court set a precedent that each "occurrence" of negligence could accrue noneconomic damages, which at that time was more than $550,000. In practical terms, that meant for each person on the care team, for each day the diagnosis was missed and for each diagnostic study based on an erroneous diagnosis, the patient could receive noneconomic damages. Though each instance claimed couldn't exceed the cap, the total "occurrences" had no limit. In essence, there was no longer a cap.

Runaway Claims

In subsequent years, the number of lawsuits and the cost of malpractice insurance dramatically increased. According to the National Practitioner Data Bank, which records physician claims, the number of claims against physicians rose by 37 percent between 2000 and 2004. In 2003, the number of frivolous claims, those that resulted in no payment, rose by 73 percent. Though no payouts occurred, the average cost of defending each claim totaled more than $11,000. For the lawsuits ended with indemnity, the average sum increased by 50 percent between 2001 and 2004.

Between 2005 and 2012, the number of claims dropped by almost 50 percent, the indemnity of paid claims dropped by 20 percent and premium decreases amounted to $27 million across the state [of Missouri].

This resulted in a dramatic increase in malpractice premiums. According to surveys by the Missouri State Medical Association (MSMA), the average increase in malpractice premiums per physician was 61.2 percent between 2002 and 2004. In a survey of every neurosurgeon in Missouri, the average increase was 116 percent between 2001 and 2003. The insurance companies were still losing money, however, and many opted to leave the state. Between 2001 and the end of 2002, a total of 24 malpractice insurance carriers stopped serving Missouri, leaving just eight.

Physicians also began to leave the state. At the end of 2002, more than 200 physicians had left or retired early. By 2004, according to an MSMA survey, 29 percent of Missouri physicians were considering leaving the state and 17 percent were considering early retirement.

Then, in 2005, Gov. Matt Blunt signed into law a bill restoring caps on noneconomic damages. These were again set at the $350,000 limit. Between 2005 and 2012, the number of claims dropped by almost 50 percent, the indemnity of paid claims dropped by 20 percent and premium decreases amounted to $27 million across the state.

Another Crisis

Now the crisis is happening again. On July 31, 2012, the Missouri Supreme Court overturned the 2005 law, declaring caps infringe "on the jury's constitutionally protected purpose of determining the amount of damages sustained by an injured party." The 4-3 decision was propelled forward with a vote from a specially appointed judge who filled in for Judge Zel Fischer.

The case in question is *Watts v. Cox Medical Center,* which alleged Naython Watts suffered brain damage attributable to negligent prenatal care. Before the Supreme Court decision, the plaintiff was awarded $3.721 million in damages. This was substantially less than the $8.5 million requested by the plaintiff and the $4.821 million that would have been awarded by the jury without the cap. Watts' attorney, whose fees were 40 percent of the award, challenged the economic cap, taking the case to the Missouri Supreme Court.

The Missouri State Medical Association, Missouri Chamber of Commerce and many state lawmakers have come out in opposition to this decision. This past legislative season, a proposal to restore caps on noneconomic damages could not pass in the Missouri legislature because of a Senate filibuster. The MSMA continues to lobby in the state legislature in anticipation that progress will be in made in 2014.

Medicine across the country is at a crossroads. In a time of tumultuous change, leaders are searching for ways to both improve care and lower costs. Trial lawyers argue caps protect bad physicians and don't incentivize safe care. Years of data from across the U.S., however, demonstrate that, when caps are removed, the number of cases filed increases but the number of successful cases decreases. This doesn't help patients; it only increases administrative costs of defending malpractice cases—costs that invariably trickle down to patients. The cost of defending frivolous lawsuits increases malpractice premiums across all medical specialties. This is analogous to prophylactically increasing an individual's car insurance expecting it will make him a better driver.

There are many other and better ways to incentivize safe care, several of which are part of the Affordable Care Act. The last repeal of a cap on noneconomic damages saw an exodus of physicians from Missouri attributable to the increases in practicing costs. With the looming shortage of primary care physicians—and health care providers in general—Missouri can't afford to have this happen again. If we don't take this opportunity to learn from the past, we will continue to repeat it, leaving doctor-less patients saddled with the consequences.

4

Malpractice Caps
Hurt Patients

Shirley Svorny

Shirley Svorny is an economics professor at California State University, Northridge, and an adjunct scholar at the Cato Institute.

Medical malpractice caps hurt patient care. Contrary to popular belief, the medical malpractice court system works well; claims in which there was no negligence tend to be thrown out. Moreover, malpractice insurers are actively engaged in identifying high-risk physicians, forcing them to pay higher premiums and giving them an incentive to provide better care. Reducing caps would reduce the incentive for insurers to police care, and would therefore result in more medical errors and damage to patients.

Congress is considering the Republican's Jobs Through Growth Act, which contains a section aimed at reforming medical malpractice by imposing caps on economic and non-economic damages similar to those in place in Texas. Texas limits non-economic and exemplary (punitive) damages in all cases, and limits what relatives can get in cases of wrongful death. An obvious disturbing consequence is that caps reduce compensation to severely-injured individuals. Caps would hurt consumers in a second way—lower damage awards would reduce medical professional liability insurers' financial incentives to reduce practice risk.

The Courts Work

Much of the protection consumers have against irresponsible and negligent behavior on the part of health care providers hinges on oversight and incentives created by the medical professional liability insurance industry. A nationwide shift to caps could result in more cases of negligence and substandard care.

Support for caps comes from individuals who see the medical malpractice system as broken, largely based on anecdotal observations. Everyone seems to have heard a story of a high verdict to a plaintiff whose claim was not valid. Yet, careful studies suggest these cases are anomalies, and the court system generally works. While there are no statistics for the country as a whole, based on the existing evidence, we can say confidently that a good chunk of initial claims (likely more than three-quarters) do not move forward because no negligence was involved. The vast majority of cases that do move forward settle.

High-risk physicians pay up to 500% more for insurance than their less-risky peers.

This means that court signals from earlier trials are clear. If court awards were random, one would expect many more cases to go to court as there would be an expectation of an award even where there was no negligence. Many cases go to court because plaintiffs think they have a case when they do not. We know this because plaintiffs rarely win; less than a quarter of all cases that go to court are resolved in favor of the plaintiff. At least one study found court findings of negligence lined up with assessments by impartial reviewing physicians.

Critics of the legal system point out that many cases of negligence are not reported or adjudicated. However, every review has found claims are concentrated among a very small subset of physicians; less than five percent of physicians are responsible for the overwhelming share of claims. Even if a large percentage of negligent actions are not reported, it would seem that the present system works in identifying physicians whose practice patterns put patients at risk.

For the system to work to reduce practice risk, malpractice premiums must be experience rated—physicians who exhibit risky behaviors must face higher malpractice insurance premiums than their less-risky peers. The conventional wisdom among health policy experts has been that experience rating does not occur. But this is not true: high-risk physicians pay up to 500% more for insurance than their less-risky peers.

Insurance companies specialize. Some only insure physicians with spotless records. Others, the surplus lines carriers, specialize in underwriting the highest-risk physicians—at any given time between two and ten percent of practicing physicians. As one broker put it, because it is so costly, being forced into the surplus lines market gets a physician's attention and motivates efforts to reduce practice risk.

Forcing Risky Physicians Out

New procedures are often left to surplus lines carriers to underwrite, adding a layer of oversight to the introduction of new procedures such as Lasik eye surgery and laparoscopic gallbladder surgery. On rare occasions, carriers deny coverage, which precludes affiliation with most hospitals and health maintenance organizations—which effectively means these really risky physicians are forced out of practice, which is exactly the desired result.

Beyond individual underwriting to identify at-risk physicians, the medical professional liability insurance industry makes significant contributions to risk reduction in other ways. Companies offer premium discounts to physicians who take risk management seminars. The Physicians Insurers Association of America's Data Sharing Project identifies risky practice patterns. High insurance premiums motivated anesthesiologists to evaluate the risk associated with their practice patterns. As a result, anesthesiology is much safer than it used to be. Some insurers visit physician offices to evaluate safety and risk.

In 1992, when Congress tried to "help" community and migrant health centers by taking on their malpractice risk, many of the health centers resisted, lamenting the loss of the risk-management services the private carriers supplied.

Under the current system, liability motivates these efforts to reduce risk. Reducing liability, as caps do, is rarely a good idea in any situation. Placing caps would reduce malpractice insurers' incentives to oversee physician practice patterns and reduce incentives to manage risk in our health care system, and make health care that much riskier for all of us.

5

Malpractice Safe-Harbor Laws Help Doctors and Patients

Zeke Emanuel, Topher Spiro, and Maura Calsyn

Zeke Emanuel is a senior fellow at the Center for American Progress (CAP) and chair of the Department of Medical Ethics and Health Policy at the University of Pennsylvania. Topher Spiro is the vice president for health policy at CAP, and Maura Calsyn is the director of health policy at CAP.

Malpractice lawsuits push physicians to use defensive medicine, ordering unnecessary tests that are expensive and may actually hurt patient outcomes. Some policy makers want to respond to this by capping damage awards. However, this is unfair to patients who experience medical malpractice and may not be able to recover the full cost of damages. A better solution is safe-harbor laws. Safe-harbor laws state that physicians are safe from a lawsuit as long as they can show that they have followed official clinical practice guidelines. Creating and implementing these guidelines and safe-harbor laws should be a policy priority.

More than 75 percent of physicians—and virtually all physicians in high-risk specialties such as obstetrics and gynecology and neurosurgery—face a medical-malpractice claim over the course of their career. While litigation costs are higher for claims that result in awards, litigation costs for claims that do not result in awards are still significant, averaging $17,130. Moreover, physicians spend an average of 11 percent of their careers with an unresolved malpractice claim, and claims that did not result in payments account for more than 70 percent of this time.

Lengthy, Costly, Frivolous Lawsuits

This length of time negatively impacts both physicians and patients. Physicians have less time to treat patients when responding to these claims and face the potential of tarnished reputations, while patients with legitimate claims must wait for resolution. These lengthy time periods can also delay implementation of quality and safety-related changes to medical practices that might prevent similar accidents from occurring in the future.

Faced with both financial and nonfinancial costs, the risk of being sued may cause physicians to practice what is known as defensive medicine, or the ordering of excessive and unnecessary medical tests, procedures, or further consultations done in part to protect the physician from accusations of negligence. Defensive medicine increases health care costs without improving health outcomes.

Patients who bring a malpractice claim must show that their physician did not meet the standard of care when treating their specific condition.

In the most recent peer-reviewed study ["The Prevalence of Defensive Orthopaedic Imaging" by Robert A. Miller et al. in 2012], orthopedic surgeons recorded in real time whether imaging was required for clinical care or ordered for defensive reasons and found that physicians ordered 19.1 percent of imaging tests and 38.5 percent of MRIs [magnetic resonance imaging] for defensive reasons. Tellingly, physicians who had been sued within the past five years were substantially more likely to order defensive imaging. The same was true for physicians who had practiced medicine for more than 15 years.

This study is consistent with many previous studies finding that 80 percent to 90 percent of physicians report practicing defensive medicine due to fears of medical-malpractice claims. In another study ["Defensive Medicine and Medical Malpractice" by the Office of Technology Assessment in 1994], in which physicians were given different clinical scenarios, the nonpartisan Office of Technology Assessment found that, on average, 8 percent of physicians chose a clinical action for primarily defensive reasons, and in certain situations, the rate was much higher. Several other peer-reviewed studies have found that malpractice costs are associated with increased health care utilization, particularly of diagnostic and imaging procedures. To the extent that this increased utilization does not improve patients' health outcomes, it represents defensive medicine.

But there is a right way and a wrong way to reduce the costs of defensive medicine. One proposal would arbitrarily cap the amount of damages that may be awarded in malpractice suits. According to the Congressional Budget Office, these caps on damages would only reduce national health spending by 0.5 percent. But while such caps would have a barely measureable impact on health care costs, they might adversely affect health outcomes. Every year about 200,000 severe medical injuries are caused by physician negligence, and with these caps in place, these patients might not be able to obtain full and just compensation for their injuries.

The Safe-Harbor Solution

To reduce the costs of defensive medicine, the Center for American Progress proposes a "safe harbor" in medical-malpractice litigation to protect physicians if they:

- Document adherence to evidence-based clinical-practice guidelines

- Use qualified health information-technology systems

- Use clinical decision-support systems that incorporate guidelines to assist physicians with patient diagnoses and treatment options

Patients who bring a malpractice claim must show that their physician did not meet the standard of care when treating their specific condition. The legal standard of care has traditionally been the local customary practice of physicians in a particular community, which is highly variable and often not supported by evidence. Under a safe harbor, guidelines would be presumed to define the legal standard of care. Patients would still be able to present evidence that these guidelines are not applicable to the given situation or that a physician did not actually follow the guidelines, and they could also use the guidelines to establish negligence by physicians.

A recent analysis of hospital data shows that defining the standard of care in malpractice cases based on nationwide medical practices reduces local variations in care. Using national practices—which are more likely to be supported by evidence—to establish the standard of care likely exposes physicians to new data and information and creates incentives to follow these national standards. In states that have adopted national practices as the standard of care, the differences in certain medical practices between those states and the rest of the nation were reduced by 30 percent to 50 percent. Eliminating the incentives to follow local customary practices that are less likely to be supported by clinical evidence increases the likelihood that patients will receive appropriate care. And the safe-harbor solution would further reduce harmful clinical variation by creating new incentives for physicians to follow specific, evidence-based guidelines.

Standards for Guideline Development

More widespread use of evidence-based clinical-practice guidelines has the potential to reduce unwarranted variation in health care practices and spending, improve the quality of health care, and improve patient safety.

Under an initiative called Choosing Wisely, 35 physician specialty groups recently released guidelines on more than 130 common tests and procedures that might be overused or unnecessary. These include MRIs for complaints of back pain, routine-stress cardiac imaging, imaging scans for simple headaches, and scans after fainting, all of which physicians may overprescribe to avert liability in the case of malpractice suits. This groundbreaking effort should inform the development of evidence-based clinical-practice guidelines.

As recommended by the Institute of Medicine, these guidelines must:

- Be based on a systematic review of the existing evidence

- Be developed by a knowledgeable, multidisciplinary panel of experts and representatives from key affected groups

- Consider important patient subgroups and patient preferences as appropriate

- Be based on an explicit and transparent process that minimizes distortions, biases, and conflicts of interest

- Provide a clear explanation of the relationship between various care options and health outcomes and provide ratings of both the quality of evidence and the strength of the recommendations

- Be reconsidered and revised as warranted when important new evidence emerges

In addition, to ensure that guidelines do not prescribe a one-size-fits-all approach, they should clearly identify any exceptions to their application.

It is critically important that guidelines be viewed as high quality, evidence based, and trustworthy. Public confidence in the guideline-development process will accelerate adoption and use of guidelines. The National Guideline Clearinghouse, or NGC, was created as a public-private partnership between the Agency for Healthcare Research and Quality—part of the Department of Health and Human Services—the American Medical Association, and America's Health Insurance Plans. As recommended by the Institute of Medicine, or IOM, the NGC should certify physician organizations—such as the American College of Obstetricians and Gynecologists and the American College of Radiology—at their request, as long as they comply with the IOM standards for guideline development. Once certified, these specialty organizations would develop evidence-based guidelines for tests and procedures in their areas of expertise. Organizational certifications should be valid for a three-year period. The NGC should also require organizations to re-evaluate guidelines at least once every three years—a frequency that research suggests is needed.

The [Affordable Care Act] strictly limits [federal] funding to projects that would not change existing state liability standards—a limitation that rules out most safe-harbor reforms.

Physicians who participate in guideline development should publicly disclose all interests, and they and their family members should be completely free from any financial conflicts of interest. In addition, guideline development should not be funded by any sectors of the health care industry, including medical imaging, device, or pharmaceutical companies.

A major cost of guideline development is systematic reviews of existing medical research. Substantial federal funding is available for such reviews by the Patient-Centered Outcomes Research Institute, or PCORI. PCORI should prioritize such reviews and make them available to physician organizations, which can then use them for guideline development. Priority should be given to specialty areas in which defensive medicine, practice variation, and medical errors are prevalent.

Beyond the Affordable Care Act

The Affordable Care Act provides federal grants for state demonstration projects to test and implement medical-malpractice reforms. But the law strictly limits funding to projects that would not change existing state liability standards—a limitation that rules out most safe-harbor reforms.

Under a separate program, known as the Medical Liability Reform and Patient Safety Initiative, the Agency for Healthcare Research and Quality funds planning and demonstration grants. While this program does not foreclose safe-harbor reforms, it has been very limited in scale. Only one planning grant has been awarded, to Oregon for the development—but not implementation—of a safe-harbor legislative proposal.

In its report on the project, Oregon estimated that implementation of a safe harbor could save about 5 percent of medical-liability costs in the state and could resolve nearly 10 percent of claims more quickly. Oregon found broad support for a safe harbor among physicians: More than 70 percent of providers said that a safe harbor would likely reduce the practice of defensive medicine. Patients would also benefit from a safe harbor because about 5 percent of injuries would be avoided if physicians followed guidelines.

At a minimum, Congress should remove funding restrictions on safe-harbor reforms and fully fund demonstration grants to states that wish to test these types of reforms.

The federal government should take additional steps to provide strong financial incentives for states to implement safe-harbor reforms. If a state implements a safe harbor and is able to reduce Medicaid costs by at least 2 percent, reduce patient injuries by at least 5 percent, and meet performance goals on the quality of care that is subject to the safe harbor, then the state would keep the entire amount of federal Medicaid savings.

The Advantages of Safe Harbor

The threat of a malpractice claim creates an incentive for physicians to mimic the practices of their colleagues, regardless of whether those treatment decisions are consistent with what clinical evidence deems necessary. In some cases, physicians may order medical tests and procedures that are unnecessary but commonly prescribed. In other cases, physicians may undertreat patients if their colleagues have not yet adopted new treatment regimes.

Proposals to limit damages awarded in these cases might lower health care costs slightly, but only with a great risk of harm to patients. Moreover, those types of reform proposals do not address the practice variations that result from the current medical-liability structure. Instead, the safe-harbor approach proposed in this brief encourages physicians to follow evidence-based guidelines, which will improve the quality of care and patient safety.

6

Malpractice Safe-Harbor Laws Won't Work

Maxwell J. Mehlman

Maxwell J. Mehlman is a professor of law and medical ethics at Case Western Reserve University.

Many people advocate safe-harbor guidelines, which would protect physicians from lawsuits as long as they followed accepted protocols when performing a medical procedure. However, drawing up such guidelines is virtually impossible, since expert opinions are often in conflict, and since those who draw up the standards often have financial interests in certain care being accepted. Furthermore, guidelines for care are already used in court cases, where they are evaluated by judges, a system that appears to work fairly well. Safe-harbor laws are therefore confusing, unnecessary, and unjust.

The idea that physicians should accept recommendations from learned colleagues on how to practice medicine is probably as old as medicine itself, but beginning around 1990, it took on new urgency in the face of rising health care costs, widespread, unjustifiable variation in practice patterns, concerns about medical errors and quality of care, and what some perceived to be perverse effects of the malpractice system. One solution put forward was practice guidelines, which the Insti-

Maxwell J. Mehlman, "Medical Practice Guidelines as Malpractice Safe Harbors: Illusion or Deceit?," *Journal of Law, Medicine, and Ethics*, 2012. Copyright © 2012 Journal of Law, Medicine, and Ethics. All rights reserved. Reproduced by permission.

tute of Medicine (IOM) defined as "systematically developed statements to assist practitioner and patient decisions about appropriate health care for specific clinical circumstances." . . .

Would Using Practice Guidelines as Safe Harbors Be Scientifically Sound?

In order for defendants to avoid liability by showing that they adhered to a practice guideline, the guideline would have to accurately describe the proper standard of care for the case in question. This was problematic in the 1990s, and a survey of recent literature shows that it is still problematic now. For example, a panel of 26 experts from multiple disciplines (health, methodological, legal, bioethics, and lay persons) convened in 2008 to study practice guidelines found that "the lack of specificity of recommendations such as the common failure to give an age after which screening [for cancer and cardiovascular disease] is no longer recommended and the variability among guidelines limits their usefulness to physicians." The panel's explanations for these deficiencies echo criticisms similar to those that had been lodged against the earlier guideline efforts: "Although every organization presumably has access to the same body of evidence to develop guidelines, screening guidelines vary from aggressive to conservative. Insufficient available evidence may be responsible for some of the variability [but] biases on the part of authors and too great a reliance on expert opinion where evidence is lacking may also contribute." The IOM recently reached a similar conclusion after surveying the guideline landscape, finding "major gaps both in the identification and development of valid practice guidelines and in the actual use of practice guidelines by the physician community."

Conflict of Interest

A major reason for the inconsistencies between guidelines continues to be bias on the part of guideline issuers. Writing in the *Archives of Internal Medicine* in 2011, one group of authors points out that "improper bias in the CPG [clinical practice guideline] production process can have a potentially more widespread adverse effect on patient care than individual practitioners' COIs [conflicts of interest]." Bias stems partly from the lack of rules about the range of expertise and viewpoints that must be employed in the guideline-writing process: "Epidemiologists and economists are often minimally represented. Different topics require different repertoires of talents. Importantly, even when it is known that areas of legitimate controversy will be covered, there is often no attempt to ensure that all sides will have reasonable opportunity to present their evaluation of the evidence and participate in the decision-making process."

It is unclear whether there are enough experts without conflicts to produce scientifically well-informed guidelines.

In addition to professional biases, personal conflicts of interest corrupt the guideline issuance process. "By favoring one test over another, or one therapy over another," [a *Journal of the American Medical Association* article from 2009] . . . points out, "guidelines often create commercial winners and losers, who cannot be disinterested in the result and who therefore must be separated from the process." Yet the guideline issuance process has failed to correct the problem. A study of the 17 cardiovascular guidelines issued most recently by the American College of Cardiology [ACC] and the American Heart Association [AHA] showed that 277 of the 498 (56%) individuals who participated in the PG [practice guideline] production process had a conflict of interest, most often as a consultant or advisory board member, followed by research grants, honoraria/speakers bureaus, and stock or other ownership. The investigators found that chairs, co-chairs, and first authors of peer reviews had an even higher rate (81%). This was particularly troublesome, the investigators pointed out, "given the fact that many of the newest ACC/AHA guideline recommendations are based more on expert opinion than on clinical trial data." . . .

Among the more notorious examples of conflicts of interest in the creation of guidelines is a guideline published in a leading cardiology journal by the Screening for Heart Attack Prevention and Education Task Force, composed of prominent cardiologists; it turned out that the publication of the guideline was paid for by a major drug company, the authors of the guideline failed to adequately disclose their financial relationships, and the guideline was never subjected to peer review. Another prominent incident was the issuance of Lyme disease treatment guidelines by the Infectious Diseases Society of America (IDSA) disagreeing with the guidelines and practices of the International Lyme and Associated Diseases Society (ILADS), especially over whether there was such a condition as chronic Lyme disease that merited long-term antibiotic treatment. The controversy became bitter, with one article describing that

> formal complaints have been filed and investigations launched against physicians treating Lyme disease on both sides of the debate. The two sides have battled in clinical trials, journals, press releases, letters, and testimony over state and federal legislation, court rooms, websites, and most recently, within the pages of their respective clinical practice guidelines. Less than a year after IDSA's revised guidelines were published, the *New England Journal of Medicine* arguably fanned the flames of dissent by publishing an article refuting the existence of 'chronic Lyme' disease. The article was written by many of IDSA's panelists. In response, ILADS issued a press release, questioning the journal's motives.

The public dispute became so bitter that Connecticut Attorney General Richard Blumenthal opened an investigation in which he concluded that "the IDSA's 2006 Lyme disease guideline panel undercut its credibility by allowing individuals with financial interests—in drug companies, Lyme disease diagnostic tests, patents and consulting arrangements with insurance companies—to exclude divergent medical evidence and opinion." Only recently have steps been taken to remedy the conflict-of-interest problem, such as rules issued by the American College of Cardiology and the American Heart Association forbidding guideline committee members from having financial conflicts, and similar rules disseminated in April 2010 from the Centers for Medicare and Medicaid Services and the Council of Medical Specialty Societies. Yet while the 2010 rules prohibit the pharmaceutical and medical device industries from paying for the development of guidelines, they do not forbid them from paying for "distribution, updating, and repurposing" of the guidelines. Furthermore, it is unclear whether there are enough experts without conflicts to produce scientifically well-informed guidelines. The cardiovascular guidelines study described earlier claimed to have found that there was still a sufficiently large pool of non-conflicted experts, but conceded that this finding "does not address the very important issue of the COIs of the professional societies that produce the guidelines, which often receive large donations from industry and rely on industry sponsorship and participation in scientific sessions." . . .

Would Using Practice Guidelines as Safe Harbors Be Sound Policy?

The foregoing section raises serious doubts about whether practice guidelines will ever be designed well-enough to serve as the standard of care. Let us assume for the moment, however, that scientifically valid guidelines produced by disinterested parties do in fact exist. And let us ignore for the time being the lingering problem of how guidelines meant to apply to population groups rather than to individuals can accommodate patient preferences and medically relevant patient differences. In other words, let us assume that there is a properly produced guideline that tells us what the standard of care is in a particular patient's case. Clearly, a physician who complies with this guideline is entitled to use it persuasively in his defense.

The medical system supplies the guidelines and the factual and scientific expertise to enable their assessment by the judicial system.

But how would we identify such a guideline? How would we know, for example, that a guideline had been properly produced and that it was based on sound scientific evidence? Moreover, how would we know that it was describing what constituted "reasonable" care, the care required by the applicable legal standard? An article describing practice guidelines in occupational and environmental medicine, for example, states that "the development of practice guidelines, if framed as recommendations for *best practices* in the prevention, diagnosis, treatment, and management of occupationally related health concerns and disability, can improve the quality of occupational medical practice and worker health and well-being." Would a guideline that described "best practices," a term often used interchangeably with "practice guidelines," be setting the legally appropriate reasonable standard of care, or a higher "optimal" standard? This may not be a problem if guidelines can only be offered defensively by defendants, since physicians would have to show that they had complied with the guideline's optimal recommendation in order to assert compliance as a defense, but that assumes that the evidentiary use of guidelines is restricted to the defendant, which, as discussed below, raises a host of practical, equitable, and constitutional objections. In any event, even if guidelines could only be used defensively, how would we know if, instead of representing a reasonable or optimal standard of care, the guideline described *substandard* care? What prevents a guideline being issued by a physician group intent on setting the bar so low that its members effectively obtained immunity from liability?

How are these issues addressed under the current system? At present, the task of ensuring that guidelines are valid descriptors of behavior that meets the applicable legal standard is a joint enterprise, involving both the judicial system and the medical system. The medical system supplies the guidelines and the factual and scientific expertise to enable their assessment by the judicial system. Contrary to complaints from critics of the jury system such as [lawyer and commentator] Philip K. Howard, moreover, it is primarily judges rather than juries who perform the validation function in the judicial system, since while juries often must determine how the defendant acted and how much weight to give the evidence of how the defendant should have acted, it is the judge who decides if the evidence is admissible and if it is conclusive enough that a jury trial to decide whether the defendant met the standard of care can be avoided.

How well is this joint enterprise performing its task? The only published study to date of cases in which the parties sought to utilize practice guidelines, an analysis by Hyams, Shapiro, and Brennan in 1996, found 28 cases in which guidelines were "used successfully" between 1980 and 1994, and cited no cases in which guidelines had been used improperly. My research assistant Kelsey Marand and I updated this study by examining cases reported between 1995 and 2011. We found a total of 24 additional reported cases. Guidelines were used successfully as a defense by defendants in 9 of the cases and by plaintiffs as inculpatory evidence in 11. In 4 cases, the courts determined that guidelines offered by plaintiffs were not inculpatory. In 4 cases, guidelines were relied upon by both parties. In all of the cases in which guidelines were successfully asserted as inculpatory, the guidelines were deemed "some evidence." In 6 of the cases in which guidelines were successfully used defensively, adherence to the guideline constituted some evidence; in 2, it gave rise to a rebuttable presumption. In their 1996 study, Hyams and his colleagues also surveyed malpractice lawyers, half of whom stated that they were aware of guidelines and a substantial number of whom stated that they gave heed to guidelines in deciding whether or not to take a case and in settlement negotiations, and there is no reason to believe that guidelines have stopped playing this pre-trial role, or that they now do so less efficiently. Based on the available data, it is perhaps difficult to be certain that the current legal/medical approach to practice guidelines in malpractice cases is running flawlessly, but the important thing is that there is no evidence that it is not running well.

The safe harbors concept rests either on an illusion or on a deception.

Could It Be Better?

Fair enough, supporters of safe harbors may say, but wouldn't their approach, in which the role of the courts in determining whether guidelines establish the standard of care would be reduced or eliminated in favor of the medical system, perform even better? The available evidence, described in this article, overwhelmingly indicates that it would not. Imagine, for example, that a medical group has issued a practice guideline and that a physician wishes to assert compliance with the guideline as a defense. If a judge did not determine if the guideline established the proper standard of care, who would? Would the fact that a medical group had issued the guideline be sufficient? What if the group in question, for example, was the Association of American Physicians and Surgeons, whose executive director states that "Comparative Effectiveness Research (CER) won't buy anything for you; it will just pay bureaucrats and researchers" and whose newsletter describes evidence-based medicine as "a greater merger of state and corporate power: [Italian fascist dictator] Mussolini's definition of fascism"?

Some commentators have suggested that authoritativeness can be achieved if the government issues, or at least certifies, practice guidelines. But others object to government-issued guidelines as anti-pluralist, anticompetitive, and an invitation to government rationing of health care. Critics of government guidelines also point to incidents like the recent controversy over recommendations for mammograms issued by the U.S. Preventive Services Task Force as demonstrating the high and potentially unsustainable political costs of government-issued guidelines. . . .

Illusion or Deception

In short, the safe harbors concept rests either on an illusion or on a deception. Either its proponents incorrectly believe that many practice guidelines exist that are capable of serving a safe harbors function or that they easily can be created and also erroneously believe that the judicial system can be substantially circumvented and still produce just results, or they know these not to be true but hope that distortions of the malpractice system and unrealistic expectations for guidelines can induce politicians to eviscerate, at patients' expense, the functions historically reserved for the law.

This leads to one final point: no other profession has gained the leverage that physicians are seeking from a safe harbors regime. Most other professions have promulgated the equivalent of practice guidelines, but in no case are their guidelines accorded automatic admissibility and conclusive legal effect, let alone one-sided application. The rules governing the conduct of lawyers, in fact, contain explicit disclaimers against even giving them a presumptive effect. As for one-sidedness, [law researcher] Michelle Mello correctly observes that "there are exceptions to the rule of symmetry, but they are few and far between, and each is justified by an important policy concern." A departure from this long-standing status quo, and especially the unfairness that a one-sided approach would impose on patients injured by malpractice, would require extraordinary justification. As this article shows, no such grounds exist.

Medical practice guidelines have an important role to play as potential evidence of the standard of care. There is no convincing reason, however, why they should be treated any differently than other forms of expert evidence, or than all other professional standards. Judges must decide threshold questions of guideline admissibility using evidence offered by medical experts subject to cross-examination so that valid guidelines can be identified. The judicial system also must determine whether evidence from admissible guidelines is conclusive, and whether or not defendants followed the guidelines. If the judge does not regard an admissible practice guideline as conclusive on the issue of the standard of care, then the fact-finder must be allowed to consider it along with other evidence introduced by both sides. Unquestionably, guidelines must be able to be introduced offensively as well as defensively. Only if the law continues to perform its time-tested functions in this way can the proper balance of power between the medical profession and the public interest be maintained.

7

Thousands of Doctors Practicing Despite Errors, Misconduct

Peter Eisler and Barbara Hansen

Peter Eisler is an investigative journalist at USA Today. Barbara Hansen is a data journalist, also at USA Today.

State medical boards are supposed to discipline doctors who have a record of medical malpractice or endangering patients. However, in practice, these boards are often extremely slow, and it may take years to sanction a doctor involved in serious malpractice cases. Hospitals, doctors, and boards are also slow to report physicians who are under investigation, making it impossible for the public to find out information about dangerous doctors. As a result, many incompetent and negligent doctors continue to treat patients, who have no way of knowing about the doctor's record.

Dr. Greggory Phillips was a familiar figure when he appeared before the Texas Medical Board in 2011 on charges that he'd wrongly prescribed the painkillers that killed Jennifer Chaney.

The Failure of State Medical Boards

The family practitioner already had faced an array of sanctions for mismanaging medications—and for abusing drugs himself. Over a decade, board members had fined him thousands of dollars, restricted his prescription powers, and placed his medical license on probation with special monitoring of his practice.

They also let him keep practicing medicine.

In 2008, a woman in Phillips' care had died from a toxic mix of pain and psychiatric medications he had prescribed. Eleven months later, Chaney died.

Yet it took four more years of investigations and negotiations before the board finally barred Phillips from seeing patients, citing medication errors in those cases and "multiple" others.

"If the board had moved faster, my daughter would still be alive," says Chaney's mother, Bette King, 72. "They knew this doctor had all these problems ... (and) they did nothing to stop him."

Mari Robinson, executive director of the Texas medical board, says the Phillips case took "longer than normal, but we followed what we needed to do (by law)." Phillips could not be reached for comment.

Doctors with the worst malpractice records keep treating patients.

Despite years of criticism, the nation's state medical boards continue to allow thousands of physicians to keep practicing medicine after findings of serious misconduct that puts patients at risk, a *USA TODAY* investigation shows. Many of the doctors have been barred by hospitals or other medical facilities; hundreds have paid millions of dollars to resolve malpractice claims. Yet their medical licenses—and their ability to inflict harm—remain intact.

The problem isn't universal. Some state boards have responded to complaints and become more transparent and aggressive in policing bad doctors.

But state and federal records still paint a grim picture of a physician oversight system that often is slow to act, quick to excuse problems, and struggling to manage workloads in an era of tight state budgets.

USA TODAY reviewed records from multiple sources, including the public file of the National Practitioner Data Bank, a federal repository set up to help medical boards track physicians' license records, malpractice payments, and disciplinary actions imposed by hospitals, HMOs [health maintenance organizations] and other institutions that manage doctors. By law, reports must be filed with the Data Bank when any of the nation's 878,000 licensed doctors face "adverse actions"—and the reports are intended to be monitored closely by medical boards.

The research shows:

- Doctors disciplined or banned by hospitals often keep clean licenses: From 2001 to 2011, nearly 6,000 doctors had their clinical privileges restricted or taken away by hospitals and other medical institutions for misconduct involving patient care. But 52%—more than 3,000 doctors—never were fined or hit with a license restriction, suspension or revocation by a state medical board.

- Even the most severe misconduct goes unpunished: Nearly 250 of the doctors sanctioned by health care institutions were cited as an "immediate threat to health and safety," yet their licenses still were not restricted or taken away. About 900 were cited for substandard care, negligence, incompetence or malpractice—and kept practicing with no licensure action.

- Doctors with the worst malpractice records keep treating patients: Among the nearly 100,000 doctors who made payments to resolve malpractice claims from 2001 to 2011, roughly 800 were responsible for 10% of all the dollars paid and their total payouts averaged about $5.2 million per doctor. Yet fewer than one in five faced any sort of licensure action by their state medical boards.

The numbers raise red flags for several experts in physician oversight, including David Swankin, head of the Citizen Advocacy Center, which works to make state medical boards more effective.

"Medical boards are not like health departments that go out to see if a restaurant is clean; they're totally reactive, because they rely on these mandatory reports—and they're supposed to act on them," Swankin says.

Not all doctors who lose clinical privileges or pay multiple malpractice claims necessarily should lose their licenses. In some malpractice cases, doctors or insurers may settle without admitting fault to avoid potentially expensive litigation.

When a disciplinary report shows up, "boards have a range of options," says Lisa Robin, chief advocacy officer at the Federation of State Medical Boards. "It could be a letter requiring that you get training, or it could be monitoring of (a doctor's) practices or, where there is patient harm, it could be something as severe as a (license) suspension or revocation."

The state boards "take their responsibility very seriously in taking actions, being thoughtful, and . . . protecting the public," Robin adds.

Decades of Concern

Concerns about medical boards' accountability date to 1986. That year, the Inspector General at the U.S. Department of Health and Human Services reported that the boards, typically comprising doctors and a lesser number of laypeople, imposed "strikingly few disciplinary actions" for physician misconduct. Several follow-up studies suggested improvements, but the reviews ended in the early 1990s after the Justice Department declared that an Inspector General would have no jurisdiction over state boards that are not funded or regulated by the federal government.

Some lawmakers disagree.

"If (medical boards) don't have proper oversight, patients will get hurt and taxpayers will get hurt," says Iowa Sen. Chuck Grassley, senior Republican on the Senate Finance Committee, which handles Medicare and Medicaid.

Early last year [2012], Grassley and a bipartisan group of senators asked the Inspector General [IG] for a "comprehensive evaluation" of state medical boards' performance. But there's been no report, and the IG's 2013 work plan doesn't mention it.

Concerns about the boards resurfaced in a 2011 study by consumer watchdog group Public Citizen. The report was based on the same National Practitioner Data Bank records reviewed by *USA TODAY*, and it reached a similar conclusion: Medical boards "are not properly acting on (clinical privilege) reports after becoming aware of them."

Yet little has changed since Public Citizen's assessment—and the congressional concern it created. Physicians with records of serious misconduct are clearly still practicing:

- A California doctor made eight payments totaling about $2.1 million to resolve malpractice claims from 1991 to 2008. The doctor's hospital privileges were restricted twice in 2007, once for misconduct that posed an "immediate threat to health or safety" of patients, and surrendered for good in 2008. No action has been taken against the doctor's license.

- A Florida doctor made six payments totaling about $1.1 million to resolve malpractice claims from 1993 to 2009. In 2004, the doctor was hit with an emergency suspension of hospital privileges for misconduct that posed an "immediate threat to health or safety" of patients, and a managed care organization took similar action in 2005. He also kept a clean license.

- A Louisiana doctor made nine payments totaling about $2.7 million to resolve malpractice claims from 1992 to 2007, and at least five payments involved patient deaths, including two young girls. In 2008, a managed care organization indefinitely denied the doctor's clinical privileges. But the doctor's license remains unrestricted.

The doctors' names are a mystery: identifying information is stripped from the Data Bank's public file. Full access is limited to medical boards, hospitals and other institutions that are supposed to weed out bad doctors.

[Dr. Greggory Phillips was] allowing a nurse to put "dangerous drugs" in the hands of patients who visited when Phillips was off and got no "adequate examination."

But the tracking system doesn't always work.

The Death of Jennifer Chaney

By the time Greggory Phillips began treating Jennifer Chaney in 2008, the Texas Medical Board had lifted the license restrictions stemming from his previous mismanagement of prescription drugs.

But more trouble was brewing. First, Phillips was caught pre-signing prescription pads, allowing a nurse to put "dangerous drugs" in the hands of patients who visited when Phillips was off and got no "adequate examination," board records show. Then, Debra Horn, a mother of two, died from an overdose of drugs Phillips prescribed.

None of that was public when Chaney's family started seeing Phillips. He treated Jennifer for poor thyroid function and residual pain from neck surgeries after a car accident, board records show. He prescribed a mix of thyroid medicine, muscle relaxants, anti-anxiety drugs and painkillers.

Just before Christmas, Chaney fell in a parking lot and re-injured her neck. Phillips prescribed a high dose of oxycodone, a narcotic more potent than morphine, board records show. He also gave her an added prescription for hydrocodone, a painkiller already included in Chaney's ongoing drug regimen—and one the board later described as "not medically indicated."

A week later, Chaney complained one evening about feeling loopy from her medications. As her husband, three sons and mother headed to bed, she stayed up to watch TV.

She was still on the couch when her mother got up in the morning.

"I noticed Jennifer was on her back, and she never slept on her back, always her side," Bette King recalls. "I didn't think anything of it; I went into the kitchen, and then it dawned on me and I went back into the den and tried to wake her up. And I couldn't."

King yelled for Jennifer's husband, who tried CPR while King called 911.

The paramedics never found a pulse. The autopsy findings: "Cause of death: mixed drug intoxication. . . . Manner of death: Accident."

As weeks passed, Phillips' problems mounted.

The medical board, which fined him $1,000 in the prescription pad case, sent notice that it was preparing to charge him with substandard care and prescription drug violations in the death of Horn a year earlier. The Horn and Chaney families each filed malpractice claims, and Phillips' clinical privileges were terminated at North Hills Hospital in suburban Fort Worth.

Yet Phillips' license remained unrestricted. He would keep seeing patients—and mismanaging their medication.

"There's no question that Dr. Phillips had (practice) violations; the question is what authority does the board have to act once those are found out," says Robinson of the medical board. "We want something to happen and we want it as quickly as it can happen. But the system isn't always set up for that. . . . That can be frustrating."

Tough Investigations, Tight Resources

There's nothing tougher for state medical boards than competency and malpractice cases.

"There are laws, there is due process and there is confidentiality, and all those things make it difficult for state medical boards to do what they do," says Jon Thomas, a surgeon and past president of the Minnesota Board of Medical Practice.

"You have to get all the facts and you have to follow the law. And it's complicated," adds Thomas, an officer with the Federation of State Medical Boards. If a board is pursuing disciplinary action, "a good lawyer representing that physician will know all the appropriate levers to push, and they push every one of them. That can take a lot of time."

The cases typically require exhaustive investigation and legal preparation—a challenge for many boards wrestling with tight budgets and short staffs.

As the recession crimped state finances, "we saw a lot of boards having to do more with less," says Robin, the federation's advocacy officer.

With disparate funding and statutory authority, various boards use vastly different approaches to keep tabs on physicians.

Florida spends more than $200,000 a year to have the National Practitioner Data Bank continuously monitor the licenses of all of its physicians, so the board is alerted automatically when malpractice cases, hospital privilege actions and other problems are reported.

In Texas, doctors must submit a Data Bank report on themselves when they first apply for a license (the Data Bank allows doctors to query their own license records), but additional checks are not required for license renewals and are done only if a need arises, such as in complaint investigations. In California, there are no set requirements for checking the Data Bank and it is not queried routinely; officials check doctors' records on an as-needed basis.

The Federation of State Medical Boards has stopped issuing medical board enforcement data.

"The states vary all over the lot in terms of the resources the boards have, whether they have good leadership, and whether they are regularly querying the (Data Bank)," says Sidney Wolfe, a physician and founder of Public Citizen's Health Research Group. "Some states do a pretty good job; a lot of them don't."

And it's getting more difficult to assess their work.

The Federation of State Medical Boards has stopped issuing medical board enforcement data that Public Citizen uses to rank the rate at which different boards discipline physicians. Wolfe says the federation wants to kill the state-by-state rankings because many boards detest them. The federation says it's figuring out how to release data that don't foster unfair comparisons between states that may have different disciplinary rules.

A Long Legal Fight

Phillips wasn't giving up his medical license without a fight.

In May 2009, nearly 14 months after Debra Horn's death, the medical board invited Phillips to a settlement conference. He accepted the board's invitation but didn't accept its deal. That left the board one option: to take the case to a judge.

In Texas, as in many states, medical board complaints are adjudicated in administrative hearings, with their own judges and all the trappings of a full-blown trial. The board spent five months gathering evidence and lining up expert testimony before filing formal charges: negligence, non-therapeutic prescribing, failure to meet standards of care and poor medical decision-making.

Then, just before the hearing, Phillips opted for mediation—and the case stalled again.

"If a physician takes advantage of every hearing, every right to trial, it takes much, much longer" to resolve a case, says Robinson, the medical board's director. "He took advantage of every hearing, everything."

At about the same time, Bette King filed her own, handwritten complaint with the board in the death of Jennifer Chaney. Another investigation was launched.

King wanted the board to exercise its power to issue an emergency suspension of Phillips' license. But the burden of proof is extremely high, and the board's staff concluded that his misconduct did not meet the two-pronged legal test for an emergency order: The conduct has to be egregious and the doctor has to be an imminent, present danger. In 2012, just a dozen cases met that standard.

By the time King filed her complaint, nearly a year had passed since her daughter's death.

"We rely on complaints to (start) investigations, and people often wait a year or more to file," Robinson says. "But to show that a physician is a present danger, it's got to be now. If we are monitoring a physician for drug use and he fails a drug test, we have recent proof that he's a danger today. If we're talking about (actions) many, many months ago, it has to go through the regular disciplinary process."

So the Phillips case dragged on. It would be another year before his mediation, and it wouldn't end there. Throughout the process, anyone who checked Phillips' status on the board's website saw a license in full force—no mention of the malpractice cases or the terminated clinical privileges, even though all of that should have been listed.

"I kept waiting for them to stop him," King says, "and they just let him keep going."

Flaws in Oversight Systems

By law, hospitals and other health care institutions—from managed care operations to public health centers—must report to the National Practitioner Data Bank when doctors lose clinical privileges in connection with investigations of substandard care or misconduct. Insurers also must report any payments in a malpractice case, regardless of whether guilt was admitted.

In Texas and many other jurisdictions, state laws require similar reporting directly to medical boards, often by doctors themselves.

The reports are critically important—hospitals and other health care organizations typically are the first to know when a bad doctor is putting patients at risk. Yet they are notorious for skirting reporting requirements when they part ways with a physician.

At the start of 2011, more than 20 years after the National Practitioner Data Bank was set up, 47% of hospitals had never reported restricting or revoking a doctor's clinical privileges, according to data from the U.S. Health Resources and Services Administration, which runs the Data Bank. Public Citizen reported in 2009 that some hospitals mask cases by giving bad doctors a chance to resign before investigations are launched, or by restricting privileges for just under the 30-day threshold that requires reporting.

But the group also found another grave problem: Hospitals' peer review committees—the internal panels of medical staff that oversee and review complaints against clinical personnel—often do a poor job.

"Much of the bottleneck in the physician discipline system is in the peer review committees," says Philip Levitt, a retired Florida neurosurgeon who served as chief of the medical staff at two hospitals. "Virtually everything of serious consequence gets balled up or blocked in the peer review process."

The peer review system is rife with bias, Levitt says, noting that doctors on the committees often are inclined to protect their colleagues—or go after those who cross or compete with them. That dynamic invites lawsuits from doctors who say they've been treated unfairly, so hospitals generally are wary of suspending even those doctors who commit egregious misconduct, Levitt adds. Instead, they tend to look for a deal to persuade the doctor to leave quietly with no misconduct finding.

To this day, Phillips' official profile on the [medical] board's website shows that he still has clinical privileges at North Hills. And the malpractice cases . . . are unmentioned.

In the rare cases where a hospital does sanction a doctor, he says, "it usually means there were really bad things going on."

In the Phillips case, North Hills Hospital says the doctor's clinical privileges ended in May 2009, not long after Phillips was fined for signing blank prescriptions. The hospital would not comment on why it parted ways with him or whether it had anything to do with misconduct that would have required reporting to the medical board.

Whatever the circumstances, the board never heard about it. "There is no public information available to suggest that a report was ever made," says the board's Robinson.

To this day, Phillips' official profile on the board's website shows that he still has clinical privileges at North Hills. And the malpractice cases, which Phillips paid to settle years ago and was required to report to the board, are unmentioned.

Tough Choices, Imperfect Deals

Based on a negotiated agreement with Phillips, the Texas Medical Board finally ordered sanctions in the Horn and Chaney cases in April 2011—more than two years after Chaney's death; three years after Horn's.

The order charged that he "prescribed excessive quantities of high dosages of controlled substances and dangerous drugs . . . and engaged in a pattern of non-therapeutic prescribing of narcotics that were being used by (both) patients at the time of their deaths by drug intoxication."

Phillips agreed to pay for independent monitoring of his practice for two years, including quarterly reviews of at least 30 patients' records. He also had to take classes to correct deficient practices, including instruction in treating chronic pain and medical record-keeping, and pay a $3,000 penalty.

But Phillips still was allowed to see patients and continue writing prescriptions.

Repeated efforts to reach Phillips for comment, including requests through his lawyers, were unsuccessful. But Jon Porter, one of his attorneys, said the sanctions were significant. He noted that paying to have a practice monitored and enrolling in the required courses can cost well over $10,000.

Still, the Phillips case wasn't over. In 2012, the board found that he'd continued to mishandle prescriptions while the Horn and Chaney investigations unfolded.

Phillips engaged in "non-therapeutic prescribing" for one patient and lacked documentation to justify the drugs he administered, the board found. In another case, he again prescribed drugs without documenting their necessity—and provided early refills without justification.

This time, the board struck a tougher deal: Phillips had to give up his certification to prescribe controlled substances.

Within a year, he'd stopped practicing, board records show. But last February [2013], the board issued another, final order that forever bars Phillips from treating patients.

Phillips "prescribed controlled substances to multiple patients without documented medical justification . . . (and) without adequate evaluation and need," the order charged, noting that he also violated rules by prescribing drugs to family and close friends.

Again, though, the sanctions were negotiated and stopped short of revoking Phillips' license, allowing him to work in "administrative medicine" with no patient contact, such as evaluating insurance claims.

The deal reflects the tough choices the board often faces, Robinson says.

"This doctor was willing to agree to something that's very strict—he'll never be in contact with patients again—or we'd have to go to trial, which could take years, and he'd be practicing for all that time," she says. "This was an immediate solution."

Phillips would have battled to the end.

"We were going to fight them (on revocation), take them to court," Porter says. "His intent was to stop practicing, but he wanted to keep his license. He wanted to go out with some dignity."

8

Feds Shouldn't Meddle with Medical Malpractice

Ramesh Ponnuru

Ramesh Ponnuru is a Bloomberg View columnist, a visiting fellow at the American Enterprise Institute, and a senior editor at National Review.

Medical malpractice laws need to be reformed in order to help doctors and patients. However, this reform should come at the state level, not from federal legislation. No one is sure what the best medical malpractice policy is; the best way to find the optimum policy is to have states experiment. Further, creating a centralized federal policy will magnify the results of any errors, and unnecessarily restrict doctors.

The idea that we should reform the way we handle allegations of medical malpractice is enjoying a new vogue.

At the end of a long cover story for *Time* magazine on high U.S. health-care costs, Steven Brill suggested that doctors who follow the best practices in the field should be shielded from liability. Peter Orszag, writing for *Bloomberg View*, argued that this policy could do a lot to reduce costs. One of the few health-care ideas that almost all congressional Republicans have agreed on, meanwhile, is caps on medical-malpractice awards.

Another proposal comes from Philip Howard: Specialized "medical courts," he says, should hear malpractice cases, just as there are courts devoted to patents, tax law and other areas where expertise matters.

Supporters of these ideas say they would do more than control costs. They would also improve the practice of medicine. Doctors would no longer order unnecessary tests, for example, to protect themselves against future lawsuits.

All of these are attractive ideas. And I don't deny that medical-malpractice law needs reform. Every doctor I know has a horror story. But lawsuits over medical care have traditionally been governed by state law—and they should continue to be.

Consequential Mistakes

The federal government should keep out of this area, first, because we don't really know the best way to reform the system. Would a legal "safe harbor" for doctors really work, or would trial lawyers find a way to get around it? Pharmaceutical companies thought that the federal drug-approval process would protect them from the whims of state courts. They thought wrong.

[One] reason the federal government should let states set their own rules is that they can do so without imposing costs outside their borders.

Even if the safe harbor proved legally effective, it could have negative effects. Doctors dislike the current system partly because it limits their ability to do what they think best for their patients, but a safe harbor for supposedly best practices could just put them in a tighter straitjacket. By placing the practice of medicine under more centralized control, the idea will magnify the effects of any mistakes the experts make.

Caps on medical liability would prevent outrageous verdicts, but a cap set too low could reduce the incentive for doctors to avoid errors. Where should the cap be set? We don't know.

The second reason the federal government should let states set their own rules is that they can do so without imposing costs outside their borders. If West Virginia chooses rules that punish obstetricians and gynecologists, some of them will move to Pennsylvania, and care will get more expensive. That's too bad for West Virginians, but it's also an incentive for them to elect legislators who will get the balance right.

Other areas of tort law don't offer this opportunity for competition and self-correction. In product-liability cases, people can sue out-of-state corporations in their own states' courts using their own states' laws. Companies with national markets have to adjust to the most demanding jurisdiction. The most punitive state or locality can thus set a de facto national policy. Federal action to stop states from hurting the rest of the country is justified: The Constitution wisely gives the federal government the responsibility to protect commerce among the states.

There's no such justification in the case of medical torts. No state can use its medical-malpractice rules to force outsiders to bear extra costs. It's true that state rules can inflate the costs of federal health-care programs (that fact helped persuade President George W. Bush to call for federal legislation to cap malpractice awards). But the federal government has voluntarily picked those costs up, and can't use its own decision as a basis for intrusions.

State Solutions

A recent study by Michael Frakes of Cornell Law School suggests that states that shield health providers from liability when they follow best practices have much lower health costs than other states. Proponents of that idea are pointing to the study to justify federal action. What it shows, though, is that states are capable of implementing such a policy on their own and can capture the benefits.

Notice that neither of those things is true in product-liability cases. No state can protect its companies from lawsuits elsewhere. And if it clamps down on abusive product-liability litigation inside its borders, much of the benefit will accrue to residents of other states.

Ken Cuccinelli, the attorney general of Virginia, is one of the few Republicans to warn his party against attempting to reform medical-malpractice laws from Washington, even though, as he wrote in 2011, "I am concerned that our legal system encourages more lawsuits than are appropriate," and even though this imposes higher medical costs. But not every problem has a federal solution, and he argued that states should fix their own laws rather than have the federal government take over the field. He's right.

9

To Avoid Medical Errors, Avoid Hospitals

Joseph Mercola

Joseph Mercola is an alternative medicine proponent, osteopathic physician, and web entrepreneur.

Hospital medical errors kill a large number of people every year. If you do end up in a hospital, it is important to have an advocate with you, and to be willing to question and ask for an explanation for each medical decision. The best way to avoid medical error, though, is to stay out of the hospital altogether. Following a healthy diet, exercising, reducing stress, and getting plenty of sleep can help maintain health and reduce the need for medical intervention.

I've long stated that the conventional health care system is in desperate need of radical change, and the findings published in a new report clearly backs up this assertion.

The US Medical System's Failures

You're probably already aware that the US has the most expensive health care in the world. In fact, the US spends more on health care than the next 10 biggest spenders combined: Japan, Germany, France, China, the U.K. [United Kingdom], Italy, Canada, Brazil, Spain and Australia.

If the US health care system was a country, it would be the 6th largest economy on the entire planet. Despite that, the US ranks last in health and mortality when compared with 17 other developed nations.

Sure, we may have one of the best systems for treating acute surgical emergencies, but the American medical system is an unmitigated failure at treating chronic illness.

I've previously posted my opinion of the so-called "Affordable Care Act" [Patient Protection and Affordable Care Act]. There is always free cheese in a mouse trap, and if you've paid any attention to how our federal government names their legislation—the name is typically the opposite of the results. Just look to the "Patriot Act" [Uniting and Strengthening America by Providing Appropriate Tools Required to Intercept and Obstruct Terrorism (USA PATRIOT) Act of 2001] or "Free Trade" agreements for confirmation, the bigger the lie the more easily it is believed.

Conventional medicine, which is focused on diagnostic tests, drugs, and surgical interventions for most ills, clearly kills more people than it saves. The lethality of the system is in part due to side effects, whether "expected" or not. But *preventable errors* also account for an absolutely staggering number of deaths.

Medical mistakes in American hospitals kill four jumbo jets' worth of people each week.

According to the most recent research into the cost of medical mistakes in terms of lives lost, 210,000 Americans are killed by preventable hospital errors each year.

When deaths related to diagnostic errors, errors of omission, and failure to follow guidelines are included, the number skyrockets to an estimated 440,000 preventable hospital deaths each year!

This is more than 4.5 times higher than 1999 estimates published by the Institute of Medicine (IOM), and makes medical errors the third-leading cause of death in the US, right after heart disease and cancer. As reported by the featured article in *Scientific American*:

> The new estimates were developed by John T. James, a toxicologist at NASA's [National Aeronautics and Space Administration] space center in Houston [Texas] who runs an advocacy organization called Patient Safety America. . . .

> [A] spokesman for the American Hospital Association said the group has more confidence in the IOM's estimate of 98,000 deaths. ProPublica asked three prominent patient safety researchers to review James' study, however, and all said his methods and findings were credible.

Avoiding Hospitals Can Be "Good Medicine"

In all, preventable medical mistakes may account for one-sixth of all deaths that occur in the US annually. To put these numbers into even further perspective, medical mistakes in American hospitals kill four jumbo jets' worth of people each week.

One of the reasons why I am so passionate about sharing *preventive* health strategies with you—tips like eating right, exercising and reducing stress—is because they can help you to stay *out* of the hospital. As a general rule, the hospital is a place you want to avoid at all costs, except in cases of accidental trauma or surgical emergencies.

According to statistics published in a 2011 Health Grades [*Healthcare Consumerism and Hospital Quality in America*] report, the incidence rate of medical harm occurring in the United States is estimated to be over 40,000 harmful and/or lethal errors DAILY! As John T. James writes in the featured report:

> . . . Perhaps it is time for a national patient bill of rights for hospitalized patients. All evidence points to the need for

much more patient involvement in identifying harmful events and participating in rigorous follow-up investigations to identify root causes.

Scientific American also quotes Dr. Marty Makary, a surgeon at The Johns Hopkins Hospital and author of the book, *Unaccountable: What Hospitals Won't Tell You and How Transparency Can Revolutionize Healthcare.* I interviewed Dr. Makary on the topic of medical errors earlier this year.

According to Dr. Makary, James' estimate "shows that eliminating medical errors must become a national priority." He also calls for increasing public awareness of "unintended consequences" associated with medical tests and procedures, and urges doctors to discuss such risks with their patients.

Part of the problem is linked to overtesting and overtreatment. And instead of dissuading patients from unnecessary interventions, the system rewards waste and incentivizes disease over health.

According to a report by the Institute of Medicine, an estimated 30 percent of all medical procedures, tests and medications may in fact be unnecessary—at a cost of at least $750 billion a year (plus the cost of emotional suffering and related complications and even death, which are impossible to put numbers on).

For the past two years, the American Board of Internal Medicine Foundation, one of the largest physician organizations in the US, has released reports on the most overused tests and treatments that provide limited or no benefit to the patient, or worse, causes more harm than good. Last year's report warned doctors against using 45 tests, procedures and treatments. This year, another 90 tests and treatments were added to the list.

To learn more, I encourage you to browse through the Choosing Wisely web site, as they provide informative reports on a wide variety of medical specialties, tests, and procedures that may not be in your best interest.

It's also important to be aware that many novel medical treatments gain popularity over older standards of care due to clever marketing, more so than solid science. . . . Recent findings by the Mayo Clinic prove this point. To determine the overall effectiveness of our medical care, researchers tracked the frequency of medical reversals over the past decade. The results were published in *Mayo Clinic Proceedings* in August [2013].

Anywhere between 40 and 78 percent of the medical testing, treatments, and procedures you receive are of NO benefit to you—or are actually harmful.

The researchers found that reversals are common across all classes of medical practice, and a significant proportion of medical treatments offer *no benefit at all.* In fact, they found 146 reversals of previously established practices, treatments and procedures over the past 10 years.

The most telling data in the Mayo Clinic's report show just how many common medical treatments are not helping patients at all—or are actually harming them. Of the studies that tested an existing standard of care, 40 percent reversed the practice, compared to only 38 percent reaffirming it. The remaining 22 percent were inconclusive. This means that anywhere between 40 and 78 percent of the medical testing, treatments, and procedures you receive are of NO benefit to you—or are actually harmful—as determined by clinical studies.

Safeguarding Your Care While Hospitalized

Once you're hospitalized, you're immediately at risk for medical errors, so one of the best safeguards is to have someone there with you. Dr. Andrew Saul has written an entire book on the issue of safeguarding your health while hospitalized. Frequently, you're going to be relatively debilitated, especially post-op when you're under the influence of anesthesia, and you won't have the opportunity to see the types of processes that are going on. This is particularly important for pediatric patients, and the elderly.

It's important to have a personal advocate present to ask questions and take notes. For every medication given in the hospital, ask questions such as: "What is this medication? What is it for? What's the dose?" Most people, doctors and nurses included, are more apt to go through that extra step of due diligence to make sure they're getting it right if they know they'll be questioned about it.

If someone you know is scheduled for surgery, you can print out the WHO [World Health Organization] surgical safety checklist and implementation manual, which is part of the campaign "Safe Surgery Saves Lives." The checklist can be downloaded free of charge here [www.who.int/patientsafety /safesurgery/ss_checklist/en]. If a loved one is in the hospital, print it out and bring it with you, as this can help you protect your family member or friend from preventable errors in care.

If you or a loved one find yourself a victim of a preventable medical mistake, Dr. Makary suggests connecting with patient communities such as:

- Citizens for Patient Safety

- ProPublica Patient Harm

Besides that, he suggests:

Ask to talk to the doctor about that mistake. If you're not satisfied, write a letter or call the patient relations department. Every hospital is mandated to have this service. They are set up to answer your concerns. If you're not satisfied with that, write a letter to the hospital's lawyer, the general council. And you will see attention to the issue, because you've gone through the right channels. We don't want to encourage millions of lawsuits out there. But when people voice what happened, what went wrong, and the nature of the preventable mistake, hospitals can learn from their mistakes.

A Healthcare System That Is a Leading Cause of Death

Medical errors are a large reason why the current, fatally flawed medical paradigm is in such desperate need of transformation. A majority of healthcare workers observe mistakes made by their peers yet rarely do anything to challenge them. A substantial portion of American doctors also suffer from burnout on the job, according to a 2012 study published in the *Archives of Internal Medicine.*

Of the nearly 7,300 doctors surveyed, nearly half had at least one symptom of burnout; 38 percent had high emotional exhaustion scores; and 30 percent had high depersonalization scores (viewing patients more like objects than human beings)—twice the rate of the general population of working adults. Clearly, this is yet another piece of the puzzle as to why US medical care is so dangerous.

All in all, leading a common-sense, healthy lifestyle is your best bet to achieve a healthy body and mind.

So what is the solution?

From my perspective there isn't any easy one, other than to simply minimize your interactions with the conventional system, as it has very little to offer anyway when it comes to prevention or treatment of chronic disease. More often than not, conventional strategies in no way shape or form address the underlying cause of your disease.

One of the reasons I am so passionate about sharing the information on this site about healthy eating, exercise, and stress management is because it can help keep you OUT of the hospital. . . .

All in all, leading a common-sense, healthy lifestyle is your best bet to achieve a healthy body and mind. And while conventional medical science may flip-flop back and forth in its recommendations, there are certain basic tenets of optimal health (and healthy weight) that do not change. Following these healthy lifestyle guidelines can go a very long way toward keeping you well and prevent chronic disease of all kinds:

1. Proper Food Choices: . . . nutrition plan. Generally speaking, you should be looking to focus your diet on whole, ideally organic, unprocessed foods. For the best nutrition and health benefits, you will want to eat a good portion of your food raw.

   Avoid sugar, and fructose in particular. All forms of sugar have toxic effects when consumed in excess, and drive multiple disease processes in your body, not the least of which is insulin resistance, a major cause of chronic disease and accelerated aging.

   I believe the two primary keys for successful weight management are severely restricting carbohydrates (sugars, fructose, and grains) in your diet, and increasing healthy fat consumption. This will optimize insulin and leptin levels, which is key for maintaining a healthy weight and optimal health.

2. Regular exercise: Even if you're eating the healthiest diet in the world, you still need to exercise to reach the highest levels of health, and you need to be exercising effectively, which means including high-intensity activities into your rotation. High-intensity interval-type training boosts human growth hormone (HGH) production, which is essential for optimal health, strength and vigor. HGH also helps boost weight loss.

   So along with core-strengthening exercises, strength training, and stretching, I highly recommend that twice a week you do Peak Fitness exercises, which raise your heart rate up to your anaerobic threshold for 20 to 30 seconds, followed by a 90-second recovery period.

3. Stress Reduction: You cannot be optimally healthy if you avoid addressing the emotional component of your health and longevity, as your emotional state plays a role in nearly every physical disease—from heart disease and depression, to arthritis and cancer.

Meditation, prayer, social support and exercise are all viable options that can help you maintain emotional and mental equilibrium. I also strongly believe in using simple tools such as the Emotional Freedom Technique (EFT) to address deeper, oftentimes hidden, emotional problems.

4. Drink plenty of clean water.

5. Maintain a healthy gut: About 80 percent of your immune system resides in your gut, and research is stacking up showing that probiotics—beneficial bacteria—affect your health in a myriad of ways; it can even influence your ability to lose weight. A healthy diet is the ideal way to maintain a healthy gut, and regularly consuming traditionally fermented foods is the easiest, most cost effective way to ensure optimal gut flora.

6. Optimize your vitamin D levels: Research has shown that increasing your vitamin D levels can reduce your risk of death from ALL causes. . . .

7. Avoid as many chemicals, toxins, and pollutants as possible: This includes tossing out your toxic household cleaners, soaps, personal hygiene products, air fresheners, bug sprays, lawn pesticides, and insecticides, just to name a few, and replacing them with non-toxic alternatives.

8. Get plenty of high-quality sleep: Regularly catching only a few hours of sleep can hinder metabolism and hormone production in a way that is similar to the effects of aging and the early stages of diabetes. Chronic sleep loss may speed the onset or increase the severity of age-related conditions such as type 2 diabetes, high blood pressure, obesity, and memory loss.

10

Medical Malpractice: Why Is It So Hard for Doctors to Apologize?

Darshak Sanghavi

Darshak Sanghavi is chief of pediatric cardiology at the University of Massachusetts Medical School in Worcester and the author of A Map of the Child: A Pediatrician's Tour of the Body.

When a medical error or a bad medical outcome occurs, patients often simply want to talk to doctors, understand what happened, and be assured that doctors did their best. Instead, however, doctors often refuse to provide information, forcing patients to go to court, which is a costly and traumatic process for everyone. Moreover, most medical errors are never uncovered or litigated. Doctors should try to learn from medical errors and from patients in order to improve care, rather than denying all errors and fighting judgments in court.

Danielle Bellerose went through hell for two years trying to conceive, undergoing nine rounds of fertility treatments before she finally got pregnant with twins in late 2003. Shortly thereafter, the then 28-year-old nurse and Massachusetts native developed a complication that required months of bed rest at home. Suddenly, on a June night nearly three months before her due date, Danielle's uterus began bleeding profusely. At 4:56 a.m. she had an emergency caesarean section at Beth Israel Deaconess Medical Center. Her daughters, Katherine and Alexis, entered the world weighing only about 3 pounds each.

Vengeance Replaces Comfort

Everything seemed to go well until the end of the first week. When Danielle and her husband, John, visited the unit, Alexis looked fine, but Katherine appeared mottled and pale. Panicked, Danielle found a nurse, and testing confirmed that Katherine was in profound shock due to necrotizing enterocolitis, a devastating intestinal complication that affects premature babies. The infant's blood had turned acidic. An X-ray indicated a tear in her bowel. Just after midnight, Katherine was taken by ambulance to Children's Hospital Boston.

Extremely premature infants such as Katherine and Alexis are entirely unprepared to live outside their mother's womb. After only 30 weeks of gestation, the newborn heart isn't fully developed, and the intestines can't easily digest breast milk or formula. At that age, a baby's brain often doesn't remember to breathe. In 1963, when President John F. Kennedy's son, Patrick, was born prematurely, the only thing to do was "monitor the infant's blood chemistry," as a newspaper of the day put it. Patrick Kennedy died after two days. By the time Katherine Bellerose was being cared for in the same hospital, however, new treatments had increased survival rates in very low birth weight infants to 96 percent.

Still, at Children's Hospital, Katherine struggled to survive. Surgeons made a last-ditch effort to save her life by removing her colon, in the hope that this would halt further damage. She failed to improve. Multiple rounds of CPR were performed.

At 5:22 a.m. on June 21, 2004, 8-day-old Katherine Bellerose was declared dead.

In the days and weeks ahead, Danielle tried to get someone to explain why no one had diagnosed Katherine's condition sooner. She made three requests to meet with the caregivers from Beth Israel. Promises were made, she says, yet no meeting materialized. Later, when Danielle contacted the hospital to get Katherine's medical records, she recalls a clerk saying no such patient had ever been treated (a problem later ascribed to a paperwork error). Danielle began to think the hospital was hiding something.

For patients seeking information, the only obvious recourse is to call a malpractice lawyer.

In time, Danielle got in touch with Lubin & Meyer, a Boston law firm perhaps best known for winning $40 million in a 2005 birth-injury case, the largest malpractice award in Massachusetts history.

Danielle's attorneys, William Thompson and Elizabeth Cranford, obtained Katherine's medical records, then asked a doctor and professional expert witness to review them. As is customary, the expert never spoke with the infant's physicians, nor did she see a need to interview the Bellerose family while preparing her report. The 10-page document, issued two years after Katherine's death, is not nuanced, even though the early warning signs of enterocolitis—such as a slight increase in the size of the abdomen and higher breathing rate—are often nonspecific and present in babies who go on to do fine. It claimed Katherine suffered a "premature and preventable death" from necrotizing enterocolitis that occurred as a "direct result" of "deviations from the accepted standards of care." Reading the report steeled Danielle Bellerose against the Beth Israel doctors and solidified her suspicion that their negligence had killed her daughter. In 2006, her attorneys filed a lawsuit against six of the doctors and nurses who had treated Katherine.

The paradox of modern medicine is that the increasing specialization that has revolutionized care has also depersonalized it. When a mistake is suspected, it may be unclear who from a team must step in to take responsibility. For patients seeking information, the only obvious recourse is to call a malpractice lawyer, whose livelihood depends on replacing a patient's desire for comfort and understanding with a need for vengeance. "In the beginning, all I wanted were answers," Danielle says. "If someone had just talked to me, none of this ever would have happened."

The longer the silence from the doctors and nurses stretched on, the more upset Danielle felt. By the 2011 trial, her disgust was so complete that, when they were testifying, she often had to leave court "to throw up."

In the end, the jury decided one doctor and one nurse practitioner were negligent—the other four defendants were determined not to be at fault—and awarded the Bellerose family $7.05 million (nearly $11.5 million with interest). It was the largest malpractice award in the state that year.

But the march to the courtroom was not inevitable. There is reason for hope that things can be done differently, even among doctors like myself who are conditioned to be suspicious of malpractice claims. Massachusetts recently enacted a law that, among other things, usually allows doctors to speak more openly to patients and families who were harmed, even apologize to them, without worry that their words will later be used against them in court. The law addresses only a small part of the problem, but it—together with data-driven efforts to find patterns of error in similar cases—is a step toward getting doctors and insurers to admit that malpractice claims often are sparked by both real failures of communication and failures in clinical care.

Hearing Patients

Something dawned on attorney Richard Boothman when he defended his first client, a Detroit surgeon, against a malpractice claim in 1981: Sometimes patients just want to be heard. The plaintiff, a woman who'd suffered a major infection after abdominal surgery, hadn't spoken with her doctor in the six years between the surgery and the trial. While listening to her doctors' testimony in court, however, the woman realized he'd done his best. She won the case, but as the jury filed out, she turned to the surgeon and said, "If I'd known everything I know now, I would never have sued you."

Later, at the University of Michigan Health System, where he is now executive director for clinical safety, Boothman put what he had learned in that courtroom to work. After a lawsuit was filed by a patient left partially blind, Boothman proposed having the patient's family and surgeon meet to discuss what had happened. The first meeting didn't go well; the patient's spouse was so upset that she immediately turned around and walked out. Boothman rescheduled and she again exited. On the third try, both sides finally started talking, and the doctor expressed his sympathies. "A transformational moment occurred," Boothman recalls. The patient later withdrew the lawsuit and then underwent a procedure that restored some of his lost sight.

The experience gave Boothman confidence in his efforts to remake the hospital network's medical liability program. In the past, all malpractice claims had been immediately outsourced to defense attorneys, who tended to fight them indiscriminately. Boothman proposed that claims first should be reviewed by impartial medical providers. If the review found a real mistake causing harm, providers were encouraged to apologize face to face, and the hospital quickly offered reasonable cash settlements.

Boothman's "disclosure with early offer" program worked well. Consider the case of Jennifer Wagner, a schoolteacher and mother of two young boys, who saw a University of Michigan doctor in 2003 for a suspicious lump in her breast. Without conducting any testing, the provider concluded it was benign. (Later the doctor said, "I guess I put the onus on the patient to monitor for changes.") Reassured, Wagner didn't mention the lump at her physical the next year. But another year later, the lump became painful, and a biopsy found advanced breast cancer. Wagner required a complete mastectomy, chemotherapy, and radiation.

In the old malpractice system—one that doctors and lawyers call "deny and defend"—parties on both sides of the case would . . . [be] girding themselves for an ugly courtroom battle.

Wagner's attorney, Thomas Blaske, sent a notice of intent to sue, alleging the missed cancer caused lost wages, shorter life expectancy, and psychological stress. Boothman's insurance analysis suggested an exposure to the hospital network of at least $3 million, and he suspected Wagner's attorneys would claim her prognosis was dire. That might reinforce and further inflame the worst fears of a young mother already plagued by anxiety.

In the old malpractice system—one that doctors and lawyers call "deny and defend"—parties on both sides of the case would have then begun girding themselves for an ugly courtroom battle. In Boothman's new system, however, five impartial doctors reviewed Wagner's case files and concluded her physician had indeed made a mistake. Within three months, Wagner and doctors sat down for an earnest two-hour meeting, where they explained she almost certainly was now cured. Wagner's lawyer, who said his role during the process changed from "warrior to counselor," remembers that as they left the meeting, Wagner turned to him and said, "I feel so good after that meeting that I don't care if I get a dime." (She eventually received $400,000 to start college funds for her sons.) Wagner's fatigue improved and she returned to teaching. "I felt like I had finally been heard," she later said. "I can't even describe how euphoric I felt when I left that meeting."

The outcome for Wagner was more humane than a prolonged malpractice trial, and also much cheaper for the insurer and hospital network. In a 2006 commentary for the *New England Journal of Medicine*, a pair of US senators pointed out that the number of pending lawsuits against the University of Michigan fell by more than half with Boothman's system, and the average time to claim resolution dropped from 21 months to 10. Despite their apparent success, however, disclosure-and-offer programs still exist only in a small number of areas. And when those two senators, Barack Obama and Hillary Rodham Clinton, proposed a new federal office to promote the programs, their bill failed.

Physicians tend to view malpractice cases as attacks that demand retaliation, not appeasement.

Malpractice Is Not Broken

Talk for a while to physicians and they'll bemoan how they're often victims of frivolous lawsuits, which are costly to both their personal reputations and the US health care system. Many of my colleagues at UMass [University of Massachusetts] Medical School and elsewhere were outraged by the $11 million judgment in the Bellerose case. The death was undeniably tragic, but did the jurors really understand anything beyond their own sympathy for the parents' suffering? The deck seemed stacked against the baby's doctors and nurses, whose complicated statements on the stand were no match for a grieving mother's sorrow.

To some extent, suspicion on the part of medical professionals is warranted. Danielle Bellerose may have filed a lawsuit as a last resort, but her attorney makes no bones about the role he needs to play in the adversarial court system. "I don't go into court to make an objective search for the truth," Thompson tells me in his office. "You know the rules: You want to win the game."

Such attitudes lead many doctors to see themselves as the real victims in malpractice cases. By the time they reach 65, data show, the vast majority of general surgeons and internists will face a malpractice claim of some type. (In my 15-year medical career, I've so far been one of the lucky ones.) Though many of these lawsuits go nowhere, the process can be intensely traumatic. Physicians tend to view malpractice cases as attacks that demand retaliation, not appeasement.

Still, there is a yawning chasm between physicians' perception of malpractice costs and the reality of them. Insurance premiums are expensive, but perhaps not as outrageous as some might guess. According to a 2012 survey by *Medical Liability Monitor*, an independent industry newsletter, base rates for OB-GYN doctors in this state are roughly $97,000 a year at one major insurer, but that is a particularly high-risk specialty. By comparison, general surgeons pay about $45,000 and internists about $15,000. UMass pays roughly $12,000 a year for my coverage.

In addition, those annual bills for doctors haven't been rising the way, say, the average person's health insurance premiums have. On the contrary, a recent analysis showed that inflation-adjusted malpractice premiums actually fell from 1975 to 2005 for 96 percent of all Massachusetts physicians. (That didn't stop the American Medical Association from declaring this a "crisis state.")

Contrary to many doctors' beliefs, there is no epidemic of frivolous lawsuits.

The specter of a lawsuit is also said to drive an increase in unnecessary medical testing and care. As the mantra goes, no doctor gets sued for doing too much. In a 2008 Massachusetts survey, doctors claimed "defensive reasons" motivated them to order roughly one-quarter of all MRI [magnetic resonance imaging] and CT [computerized tomography] scans, one-quarter of all referrals to specialists, and 13 percent of hospitalizations.

But studies show that doctors order a lot of questionable testing and treatment even when malpractice risks are very low. On top of that, Harvard researchers recently estimated that all medical liability costs add only 2.4 percent to national health care spending anyway (though, to be fair, that percentage still represented more than $55 billion in 2008).

Contrary to many doctors' beliefs, there is no epidemic of frivolous lawsuits. In 2006, the *New England Journal of Medicine* published an analysis of 1,452 randomly selected malpractice cases from around the country. It came as a surprise to most readers that 97 percent involved a medical injury, while almost two-thirds involved a mistake on the part of health care professionals. Looking at case outcomes, the researchers concluded that although the malpractice system is not perfect, it "performs reasonably well." In fact, when doctors make an actual mistake, the system is slightly biased in their favor.

The misleading image of the doctor besieged by bogus lawsuits dangerously obscures an important fact: The vast majority of major medical errors never see the light of day. A classic 1991 study found that only about 2 percent of patients harmed by medical negligence filed a claim. According to a spreadsheet I was given, Harvard-affiliated hospitals were the target of only 90 malpractice claims relating to children between 2006 and 2010, a period when doctors racked up millions of patient encounters. The vast majority of the medical care at these hospitals is superb, to be sure, but it strains credibility to think that any major academic center makes a harmful mistake so rarely (especially when a 2010 study showed that 15 percent of all hospitalizations result in preventable harms).

The remarkable thing, therefore, isn't that Americans file too many malpractice lawsuits, it's that they file so few. Some physicians courageously fess up and communicate with compassion after an error and defuse a patient's anger. At the same time, some appear to sweep errors under the rug. For example, I became aware that a serious misread of an ultrasound led to a patient's death at a large medical center. When I reported the matter to a senior administrator there, I was asked not to engage the matter further.

The bitter fact is that there is no appetite in the medical community to come clean preemptively about every medical error.

Like many physicians, I know about dozens of such cases. While I worked a stint at a health center for underserved patients, a provider evaluated a young woman with intermittent abdominal pain and discharged her back to school, missing the fact that she was giving birth. Later in the day, the patient—who didn't know she was pregnant—delivered her baby alone in her bedroom, panicked, and shut the baby into a suitcase. The baby died, the mother was propelled into the criminal justice system, and the provider faced no major consequences.

Last August [2012], Massachusetts enacted reforms that usually make doctors' apologies inadmissible in court, require claimants to file "letters of intent" before suing, and impose a six-month waiting period to allow doctors and patients to work out the matter. The law might pave the way for earlier, more amicable settlements.

But the bitter fact is that there is no appetite in the medical community to come clean preemptively about every medical error. The list of them is just too long. No major reforms, including those just passed here, are truly proactive, since they all still require patients or families to call a lawyer before anything happens.

And so we have our peculiar, perverse system. Injured patients are often left in the dark unless they decide to act. Most never do. But a few call an attorney, the medical system springs to respond, and the battle eventually ends with much collateral damage and expense. Progressive proposals seek to take a case like that over the death of Katherine Bellerose, de-escalate it, and resolve it out of court. That's a good thing for patients and doctors, and such programs deserve wide adoption. The problem is, they would still not be enough.

The key [to reducing malpractice claims] . . . was that the doctors didn't see lawsuits as nuisances to be stamped out, but as "the tip of the iceberg" of substandard medical care.

Lawsuits as Symptoms

Those on the cutting edge of malpractice reform focus on studying the 2 percent of mistakes that enter the court system, in hopes of applying what they find to the 98 percent of errors that quietly send tens of thousands of Americans to the grave each year. These innovators parse thousands of claims and, mostly hidden from view, mine the data to find ways of stopping errors from occurring in the first place.

At a conference room in Cambridge overlooking the Charles River, Dr. Luke Sato and a colleague project a spreadsheet on the wall. Sato oversees a team that studies data in malpractice claims at CRICO, or the Controlled Risk Insurance Company, a not-for-profit consortium that insures all claims from Harvard-affiliated hospitals. Over the past 30 years, the team has created a taxonomy of medical errors, with hundreds of codes for everything from "failure to identify provider coordinating care" (CS1001) to "policy/protocol not followed" (AD1026).

This spreadsheet is an analysis of the records from a deceased young girl, whose parents sued doctors for allegedly failing to diagnose and treat her heart defect. For every claim such as this one, an impartial medical expert reviews the patient's chart for mistakes. (Interestingly, the only way for a patient to obtain such a case review is by having a lawyer file a malpractice claim.) In the girl's case, the review found six specific contributing factors. Each was coded, recorded, and added to the data on similar cases.

This concept was employed in the 1980s by the American Society of Anesthesiologists, whose specialty was being buffeted by massive jumps in malpractice premiums and waves of bad publicity. Anesthesiologists created a national database of closed malpractice claims and fed them into a computer at the University of Washington. Surprisingly, it turned out that many patients were dying of the same mistake: incorrectly inserted breathing tubes. A simple technological fix—monitoring the patient's oxygen level with a sensor—was made a standard of care in 1986. Lawsuits against anesthesiologists dropped dramatically.

The key, says retired CRICO president John McCarthy, was that the doctors didn't see lawsuits as nuisances to be stamped out, but as "the tip of the iceberg" of substandard medical care. McCarthy immediately saw promise for his hospitals in this data-driven approach. In the 1990s, when many doctors were sued for missing breast cancer, CRICO analyzed claims and discovered that doctors had no uniform approach to monitoring lumps. McCarthy's team developed a standard breast care algorithm for Harvard hospitals and offered doctors who learned the procedure discounts on their malpractice insurance premiums. As a result of the changes, he says, there was "almost complete resolution" of related litigation in the Boston area. . . .

CRICO has replicated its results in other medical situations. When its data showed doctors getting hammered for obstetrical complications, largely as a result of teamwork problems, CRICO created a team-training course and gave premium discounts to enrollees. Claims soon fell by 50 percent. Then data showed that 20 percent of Boston-area claims involved communication breakdowns, and CRICO found that surgical trainees didn't want to appear weak by contacting senior physicians for help. In response, a "trigger card" automatically notified senior physicians of certain alarming developments, relieving trainees of the responsibility. The list of improvements goes on. Overall, CRICO's paid claim rates now are less than half that of insurers in California and one-fourth of those in New York and Pennsylvania. Most notably, CRICO improved care for all patients, not just those who filed lawsuits.

Since 1990, CRICO has been analyzing claims from 520 health systems around the country that employ more than 75,000 physicians. The database it has created—the Comparative Benchmarking System—is the most detailed repository of malpractice data in the world. "This can transform the system of care," says Mark Reynolds, CRICO's current president. "If I had to be bold, I'd say our data mining largely explains why our claims rates are lower than other regions.'"

Thinking of Katherine Bellerose, I asked CRICO to examine necrotizing enterocolitis claims in the repository from the past decade, a data set it turns out no one had previously asked for. Two weeks later, a member of the team e-mailed me a detailed spreadsheet containing more than two dozen cases (none included information that would identify patients).

The CRICO team tagged 137 errors that could be grouped into 35 categories. There were several patterns among the cases. In more than half, there was a delay in ordering X-rays or other tests. In a third, the team overlooked the possibility of enterocolitis in spite of clinical signs. In a quarter, there were communication problems among doctors, often related to shift changes. There were instances of "failure to question" an incorrect medical order and others where staff "failed to respond" to repeated concerns from patients.

Twenty to 30 percent of very low birth weight infants who develop necrotizing enterocolitis die from it—that mortality rate hasn't budged in more than a decade, despite advances in medical technology. The claims data won't be a miracle fix, but they do make a constructive suggestion for improvement: Standardize care. Neonatal doctors need to agree on the early signs of the condition and on when to use antibiotics and order tests. Then they need to improve how they interact with each other and with families. The data might not tell us exactly how to fix problems, but they do show how the care of preemies with necrotizing enterocolitis repeatedly goes wrong.

Another Chance

In late 2011, Danielle Bellerose sat with me on a bench in front of her modest Colonial home north of Boston.

In the time after her daughter's death, she told me, all she wanted was to meet with her baby's doctors and be reassured that they had done all they could. But they never spoke again.

For her, seeking legal redress was "not a therapeutic process," and the stress led to years of depression and therapy. Awaiting trial, she lacked any sense of closure—she could never even bring herself to put a headstone at Katherine's grave. In the meantime, her anger at the doctors and nurses festered.

In medical training, doctors are taught the importance of listening to patients and their families, but the lessons are often too easy to forget. If Danielle Bellerose felt her daughter's doctors and nurses responded better to her questions, they might have avoided a major malpractice suit. I also told Danielle about the CRICO analysis—like most, she was unaware such processes existed—and she seemed pleased to know that some improvement in future care might come from her daughter's death.

So it's not too late: Katherine Bellerose and other patients are still telling their stories, just now in a different way. We have another chance to listen.

11

The ACA Will Have a Major Impact on Medical Malpractice Law

Alexander C. Davis

Alexander C. Davis was the editor of the law review at the University of Louisville Louis D. Brandeis School of Law. He is currently an attorney at Jones Ward PLC in Louisville, Kentucky.

The Affordable Care Act (ACA) will change medical malpractice in a number of important ways. First of all, the law calls for programs to explore different ways of reforming the medical malpractice system. In addition, the ACA will have many indirect effects on medical malpractice. Some of these will be related to the fact that many more people will be insured and seeking medical care, which will change insurance premiums and litigation in uncertain ways. The ACA should also reduce reliance on emergency room visits and make patient records more easily available, both of which could have an important effect on malpractice lawsuits.

Critics of the Affordable Care Act [ACA, officially the Patient Protection and Affordable Care Act] claim that one of the legislation's downfalls is a lack of meaningful changes to the rules that govern medical malpractice. They argue that efforts to limit a patient's right to recover damages for injuries—also known as "tort reform"—would lead to lower healthcare costs for consumers, and reduced insurance premiums for physicians and other medical providers. This proposition is open to debate, with widely divergent statistics on both sides of the argument. What is not debatable, however, is that if the U.S. Supreme Court upholds the ACA in its entirety, the law *will* actually lead to major changes in the landscape of medical malpractice litigation in the United States.

Change Will Happen

Change will happen for two reasons. First, it will happen because the ACA does contain some modest legislative measures that will affect medical malpractice. For example, one change in the law extends malpractice coverage to employees and others who work in free clinics under the Federal Tort Claims Act. This will create a new layer of protection for some providers, but it also will make them more attractive targets for lawsuits. Another example is a pilot program that will allocate $50 million in state-level funds for "alternatives to current tort litigation for resolving disputes over injuries allegedly caused by health care providers or health care organizations." The state-based initiatives are not expected to generate major changes in the healthcare industry, partly because the pilot programs are not allowed to curb patients' ability to sue medical providers. Another component of the ACA that could affect malpractice is an effort to regulate excessive increases in insurance premiums for doctors. The pilot program and other components of the ACA still will affect medical malpractice overall. Small change does not mean no change at all.

The second and more important reason that the ACA will change malpractice litigation can be traced to the indirect impact of the other substantive changes the law will bring to the nation's healthcare system. For example, millions of newly insured patients will alter the pattern of malpractice lawsuits because more people will be receiving medical care, and some of that care will be negligent. Changes in the way medical expenses are reimbursed by the government also will affect malpractice litigation, as will the mandate to expand the use of electronic medical records and add new insurance regulations. . . .

It appears that physician and provider liability will not be dramatically increased as a result of the ACA, and it could be lessened.

Tort Reform Pilot Projects and Other Direct Changes in the ACA

The most direct impact of the Affordable Care Act on medical malpractice law is the $50 million in funding it provides for state programs that will explore alternatives to current tort law as it relates to medical malpractice. The money will be made available in the form of state grants over a five-year period. States that want to receive grant money must develop a program that reduces medical errors by "encouraging the collection and analysis of patient safety data related to disputes. . . ." Although the pilot programs are not expected to result in major sweeping changes, their goals directly target some of the most pressing issues in the health-care system, such as resolving disputes efficiently, reducing medical errors, and enhancing patient safety. They also aim to "improve access to liability insurance" and show patients alternatives to filing lawsuits. The alternative methods for resolving disputes can be funded by public or private money, or a combination of the two. This effort to explore alternatives to the current tort system could provide valuable information over the next few years. Supporters of more widespread tort changes downplay the benefit of the ACA's pilot program, saying it is not designed to address the root problem of abusive tort litigation. One commentator pointed out that the government official in charge of supervising the program is a former trial lawyer for plaintiffs, and stated that the handful of programs receiving funding so far have been "ineffectual" in terms of addressing litigation costs and profiteering lawyers. This is a premature judgment at best. It is simply too soon to tell how much of an impact the programs will make because the grants have only been available since the beginning of fiscal year 2011. It could very well be that after that five-year period is over there have been a host of innovative solutions that will pave the way for future changes. In fact, one grant program in Missouri is already drawing praise for its focus on reducing birth injuries by improving communication and teamwork between healthcare providers. Furthermore, there is reason to believe that innovation is happening apart from the grant projects, as providers explore ways to reduce less than optimal outcomes.

Five *Indirect* Impacts of the ACA on Medical Malpractice

The Affordable Care Act also includes dozens of other details covering everything from children's access to hospice services to new tax regulations for prescription medication. The changes will cost billions of dollars in taxpayer funds, but they also could address five of the most pressing problems in healthcare that affect malpractice litigation: the burden of uninsured patients on hospital emergency rooms; the large number of Americans who lack health insurance; the need for better electronic medical records; the growing disconnect between the cost of medical care and the quality of that care; and a lack of regulations for the insurance industry.

These changes likely will have a bigger impact on medical malpractice litigation than the pilot programs mentioned above. The changes are, however, more difficult to ascertain on the surface. It also is harder to tell if the changes will lead to more lawsuits, fewer lawsuits, or different kinds of verdicts.

Overall, however, it appears that physician and provider liability will not be dramatically increased as a result of the ACA, and it could be lessened.

The "ER" Problem and Malpractice Litigation

Heavy reliance on emergency rooms [ER] by sick Americans is a pressing problem. Total U.S. spending on emergency care stood at $47.3 billion in 2008, a figure that has grown rapidly in recent years as uninsured patients turn to emergency rooms as an alternative to routine doctor's visits. Indeed, the number of emergency department visits in 2009 increased to 136 million nationwide, up 12 million from the previous year. The increases are even more pronounced at some hospitals that specialize in serious trauma. For example, University Hospital in Louisville, Kentucky, saw total ER visits jump to 58,010 in 2011, a 75 percent increase from 2006.

When patients use emergency rooms as a substitute for their routine medical needs, the consequences can often be deadly. A visit to the ER costs vastly more than a trip to a doctor's office, and those costs can be multiplied when an individual has delayed treatment of an ordinary illness. This, in turn, leads to potentially higher verdicts in cases where malpractice is committed, because the injuries are more severe. Hospital emergency rooms also do not have the luxury of deciding which patients to treat, due to the requirements of the Emergency Medical Treatment and Active Labor Act. Emergency care also can be a hotbed for overcharging and unnecessary procedures, sometimes known as defensive medicine. In fact, some argue that nowhere do doctors face more pressure to overtreat than in the ER, where life-and-death decisions are part of the daily routine. Emergency room doctors also are among the most likely physicians to be sued for malpractice, along with obstetricians, surgeons, and internists.

The Affordable Care Act aims to lower this reliance on the ER by extending insurance coverage to more Americans. This, in turn, will cut down on the number of people who are driving to the ER instead of seeing a doctor for a routine checkup. Litigation involving emergency care obviously will not go away, but it could very well be reduced for poor patients.

Recent research shows that poor people in general are less likely to sue their doctor.

Expanding Insurance Coverage May Lead to Fewer Lawsuits

Perhaps the largest potential shift in malpractice is the introduction of millions of newly insured patients under an expanded Medicaid system. Under the ACA, individuals who earn up to 133 percent of the federal poverty guidelines will be eligible for Medicaid, the government-insurance program for the poor. This expansion alone is expected to add between sixteen and twenty million new people to the nation's Medicaid rolls. This expansion of insurance coverage—from both Medicare and from sources such as the individual mandate—will send ripples into the malpractice industry that extend far beyond emergency rooms. For example, one area where the ACA could affect physicians is in preventive care for pregnant women. If fewer people are uninsured, especially the young and healthy, there is a greater chance that those people will receive earlier diagnosis and treatment, particularly when it comes to prenatal care, which will lead to fewer adverse outcomes such as birth injuries.

The expanded number of insured patients also may translate into an increase in the rate of non-physicians providing medical care to patients. This is partly due to the ongoing shortage of primary-care physicians, although the numbers vary by locality. The impact of this trend cuts in two directions. On one hand, it could mean lower malpractice rates if the physician shortage is relieved, but on the other hand it could lead to an increase in bad outcomes due to a lower level of training among non-physicians and more diagnostic errors. The interaction of the ACA with this trend is difficult to gauge either way. Even without the expanded insurance coverage, the move toward non-physicians providing care at retail clinics is unfolding as a result of market forces and consumer demand.

Supporters of tort reform might argue that expanded insurance coverage may lead to more malpractice litigation due to the sheer number of additional patients receiving care, and the added stress on the medical system. The actual outcome, however, could be the opposite. Recent research shows that poor people in general are less likely to sue their doctor, partly because they lack access to legal resources and are less likely to have enough money to initiate a malpractice claim. Even notwithstanding this tendency, the potential for additional strain on doctors and hospitals is not a justification for reduced legal rights. The more appropriate answer is better training for physicians, increased enrollment in medical schools, expanded facilities, or a combination of all of the above.

Electronic Medical Records

The Affordable Care Act makes a number of changes to laws governing how medical records are created and maintained. For example, funds are provided to create statewide electronic databases of immunization records. Another component of the law, titled Strengthening Public Health Surveillance Systems, appropriates $190 million annually to develop and maintain an "information exchange" among state and local health departments for information about disease prevention and other epidemiological issues. The law also provides training to long-term care facilities to transmit prescription and patient information electronically, and it requires increased use of electronic health records by doctors and other providers. Finally, the law creates standardized billing procedures for providers, and requires health plans to adopt rules for the confidential exchange of health information. These efforts will lower costs, reduce medical errors, and improve the quality of care.

These improvements make sense. Technology to make these changes is readily available, and the healthcare industry is one of the last segments of the nation's economy that still relies on paper records. A patient who is referred by a primary care provider to a specialist such as a surgeon should be able to have his or her records transferred seamlessly from one provider to the other. There could be minor problems in the early stages of transition to a fully electronic system, but with adequate planning and training there is a good chance that medical errors can be reduced. For examples, a truly uniform and transferable system of electronic health records would greatly reduce the potential for cases in which a doctor is not fully aware of a patient's medical history. It also would make it easier for a doctor to make a diagnosis based on a patient's past health issues, and it could lower the need for tests that have already been conducted by other providers.

Providers will be able to form Accountable Care Organizations (ACOs) to coordinate treatment and achieve cost savings.

Quality and Cost: "Defensive Medicine" and Other Myths

Supporters of tort reform argue that medical malpractice litigation is driving doctors away from practicing medicine, and in some cases forcing them to practice so-called defensive medicine which drives up costs for everyone. One study, for example, showed that the practice of defense medicine—using unnecessary tests and procedures to ward off the threat of litigation and deal with insurance liability premiums—costs $50 billion a year. But it is maddeningly difficult to put a real number on the issue. There is little definitive information on the subject, and estimates can vary widely. Case in point: another study on defensive medicine that showed the cost may be as high as $650 billion a year. Doctors also seem to be convinced that they are practicing defensive medicine, with 92 percent of physicians in one survey reporting that they had used unnecessary medical procedures in the previous 12 months to avoid a lawsuit, even though very few physicians are ever successfully sued for malpractice. Government studies also show that it is difficult to tell whether these tactics amount to defensive medicine because there are other factors behind the utilization rates of various procedures, not the least of which is their revenue-enhancing potential for the physician.

Finally, studies that do attempt to examine so-called defensive medicine and other tort-related issues often fail to take into account the economic benefits of the nation's civil tort system, such as reducing accidents and injuries, redistributing wealth from corporations to individuals, and reducing the need for government regulation. They also often do not take into account the impact of factors such as the growing popularity of retail health clinics, which reduce costs and improve access to medical care, but also may increase the possibility of provider liability.

The Affordable Care Act does a number of things that will address some of the above financial problems by connecting quality of care with cost of care. For example, providers will be able to form Accountable Care Organizations (ACOs) to coordinate treatment and achieve cost savings. Data from the ACOs will be publicly available, which could provide ammunition for plaintiffs' lawyers to establish liability, but also could act as a deterrent against errors and unnecessary testing.

Physicians have already been privy to some of this information, but it only makes sense for patients to share in that access. For example, through the Physician Quality Reporting Initiative, the law will make available to the public, via a Web site, statistics on an individual doctor's patient outcomes, coordination of care, and overall efficiency.

The ACA also does things to reduce costs that will be far more effective than any changes to the tort system. Perhaps the most visible change is the effort to reduce Medicare and Medicaid fraud, which is expected to return $17 to taxpayers for every $1 invested. Additional money will be saved by increased use of generic biologic agents, and by removing unnecessary payments to Medicare Advantage plans. Finally, the ACA's creation of a new research institute will give physicians and other care providers new tools to study the effectiveness of various medicines and procedures. The institute's work, at least in theory, should allow providers to pick the most cost effective and efficient means of administering medical treatment.

The Need for Tighter Regulation of Insurers

To be certain, the rising cost of health care in the United States is one of the nation's biggest problems. Some people believe that a high number of medical malpractice lawsuits is part of the problem. They argue, in part, that placing limits on a patient's ability to recover in a medical malpractice action will lead to lower insurance premiums for physicians because insurers and their customers will not be exposed to multi-million dollar awards for pain and suffering. But evidence shows that tort reform efforts rarely, if ever, lead to lower insurance premiums. Some changes, such as caps on pain and suffering, may translate into lower verdicts for plaintiffs but they do nothing to lower the cost of litigating because hospitals and doctors still must pay for the cost of defending litigation. Furthermore, some tort reform efforts have been deemed unconstitutional on the grounds that they infringe on court rules and how plaintiffs may bring a case to trial. In Georgia, for example, the state's highest court struck down a $350,000 cap on non-economic damages in medical malpractice cases.

Experiments with tort reform in places such as Florida and California show that the biggest driver of cost is not malpractice, but low investment returns for insurers and decisions made by insurance companies themselves. For this reason, what the marketplace needs is not changes to tort law, but more regulation of the insurance industry. Fortunately, the Affordable Care Act contains some changes that will lead to achievements in this area. These changes include a "pay for performance" initiative that will dock reimbursements for care providers who fail to meet minimum standards, and insurance exchanges that will promote quality and safety. These and other changes provide a set of powerful incentives for health plans to focus on patient safety, and move away from the current model where providers can still receive money for botched procedures, and then collect additional funds to provide follow-up care to correct their errors.

12

The ACA Will Have a Minor Impact on Medical Malpractice Law

Heather Nicole Seigler

Heather Nicole Seigler is a litigation attorney with State Farm Insurance in the Los Angeles area.

The Affordable Care Act (ACA), officially named the Patient Protection and Affordable Care Act, was initially supposed to address the broken medical malpractice system. However, due to red tape, bureaucracy, and political disagreement and fear, the final bill did little to address the problem. The only provisions in the ACA regarding medical malpractice are grants encouraging states to experiment with solutions. This is an inadequate response given the large scale of the problem. Moreover, since the ACA is unlikely to be altered substantially in the near future, medical malpractice reform has been put off for the foreseeable future.

When the PPACA [Patient Protection and Affordable Care Act] went through various committees, incarnations, and drafts, Congress utilized President [Barack] Obama's list of guidelines and proposed various ideas that touched on, and sometimes expanded, President Obama's goals. . . .

An essential difference between the different plans was the attention to medical malpractice reform needed. In the

Heather Nicole Seigler, "Affordable Care and Medical Malpractice—How Two Broken Health Care Systems Will Only Get Worse Without Better Compromise," ExpressO, 2013. Copyright © 2013 Heather N. Seigler. All rights reserved. Used by permission.

Patients' Choice Act of 2009 the cost containment plans would create independent expert panels or state "health courts" to review cases and render decisions, provide bonuses to states that enact medical malpractice reforms and limit malpractice lawsuit rewards. The National Health Insurance Act would have created a cost control mechanism that included an analysis of the impact on medical malpractice claims and liability insurance on health care costs. From these failed bills, it is clear that medical malpractice reform was contemplated within Congress, however, the only medical malpractice measure to end up in the PPACA was a five-year grant to the states to develop, implement, and evaluate alternatives to current tort litigations.

The implementation of medical malpractice five year grants to states to develop, implement, and evaluate alternatives to current tort litigations, cited "the sense of the Senate that—(1) health care reform presents an opportunity to address issues related to medical malpractice and medical liability insurance." These grants "encourage" development and testing of alternatives to existing civil litigation systems and tell Congress to "consider" establishing State demonstration programs to evaluate alternatives to resolving medical malpractice claims. This grant system will allow the Secretary of State to authorize award demonstration grants over five years to states who implement programs that test and evaluate potential changes to the medical malpractice litigation system. . . .

There are many questions associated with a total health care re-haul—what role should the government take? Should there be health plans? How much should it cost?

No Progress

While Section 10607 of the PPACA does account for each prong of the medical malpractice system by asking the grant committees to consider programs that promote patient safety and reduce medical error (the Medical prong), creates alternative dispute resolution (the legal prong) and helps reduce medical error (the malpractice insurance prong), it does nothing to actually change anything. The PPACA merely pays the States to *consider* making changes to their plans, and does not require any patient or doctor to opt in to whatever plan is proposed by the grant-funded committee. The PPACA missed the opportunity to revamp the court system with the Patients' Choice Act's "health courts" and control costs and maintain a real analysis of just how much the medical malpractice system costs the country's health care with The National Health Insurance Act. It should have taken the cues from those proposals to actually create solutions to problems, not merely contemplate the solutions.

The PPACA likely included medical malpractice reform because conservative politicians often believe tort reform will provide the means for health care reform, where liberal politicians believe trending toward a more socialized health care plan will provide the best means for health care reform. When it comes to bridging the gap between conservatives desiring tort reform and liberals desiring universal health care, the solution seems simple: combine universal health care with medical malpractice reform. While the PPACA attempted to create such a solution, it failed on both accounts.

Missed Opportunity

The problem is, as President Obama stated, the best means to change the health care system is not to completely change it, but to "fix what's broken and build on what works." As pointed out in the *New England Journal of Medicine* in 2005, there are many questions associated with a total health care re-haul—what role should the government take? Should there be health plans? How much should it cost? What mechanisms of accountability are built in the system to ensure resources are used well? There are no answers that come immediately to mind. When there have been answers, they have been deemed too complicated.

For example, in 1992, Hillary Rodham Clinton led the President's Task Force on Health Care Reform, which sounded a lot like the initial Obama Administration-outlined goals of the PPACA. The Task Force presented the 1,300 page, extremely detailed, Health Security Act in October of 1993. The government would make it mandatory for all citizens to have health insurance, and would create a means for people to get it. The new system would provide health care to all citizens and lawful residents of the United States, who would receive health security cards. Under this system, Medicaid would have been folded into the new health care insurance system and the government would contract with a number of health plans to create community-rated premiums based on the least expensive plans in the region. The system would have guaranteed the affordability of health care, regardless of malpractice costs, because it would be completely governmentalized. However, when the true extent of the plan came out (a complete overhaul of the healthcare system), the Task Force came to an end. It was deemed too complicated.

The failure of such a thoroughly researched, well-thought out plan is the perfect example of just how much modern politics gets in the way of real change. The best healthcare reform plan, which was strategically created to effect change from the 20th through the 21st century and beyond, was deemed too complicated and doomed to stall on the committee floor. Was it fear of the unknown? Was it fear that an overhaul of the system would be extremely expensive and even after all of the expense it might fail? The reality was the Health Security Act would not have passed through the House and Senate. The questions regarding the Act's potential to succeed or fail were barely even considered. The complete overhaul the Task Force called for was too extreme for those hesitant to vote for a bill that would so completely change the healthcare system. Without gaining support from those on the fence then and now any bill with similar weight and magnitude is also doomed to fail. Simply put, extreme change seems impossible when the potential change has to better the country is not considered *before* a bill's popularity is.

The real change in the PPACA, as a whole and specific to medical malpractice, was lost to moderation.

Red Tape

President Obama was more fortunate to be elected in a time when healthcare reform was a popular hot-button issue. However, the lofty goals of PPACA were also stalled by bureaucratic red tape. In committees, and throughout the process of passing the PPACA, President Obama's best laid plans were weeded out. Thus, the PPACA failed to create universal health care. It failed to even make an optional federal government-run insurance, even though it was part of President Obama's initial plan, and part of earlier drafts. The PPACA also failed to create any kind of medical malpractice reform at all. Instead the states were tasked to consider creating alternative dispute resolution programs that would be prototypical and optional for doctors and patients to utilize. On both accounts, as President Obama even stated: "nothing in our plan requires you to change what you have." While these words were meant to be encouraging to people who were scared of or against health care reform, the fact of the matter is President Obama admitted that his plan had the potential to change everything by creating a government-run, inclusive insurance program (as indicated in his outlined plans and earlier drafts), and yet ended up changing nothing substantial.

The inherent weakness of the PPACA was that the bureaucratic drafting process compromised it. President Obama established his vision, and that vision was slowly eroded due to the political moderation process required to get it to pass.

The contemporary form of moderation, however, simply assumes government growth (i.e., intervention), which occurs under both parties, and instead concerns itself with balancing the regulatory interests of various campaign contributors. The interests of the insurance companies are moderated by the interests of the drug manufacturers, which in turn are moderated by the interests of the trial lawyers and perhaps even by the interests of organized labor, and in this way the locus of competition is transported from the marketplace to the legislature. The result is that mediocre trusts secure the blessing of government sanction even as they avoid any obligation to serve the public good. Prices stay high, producers fail to innovate, and social inequities remain in place.

The real change in the PPACA, as a whole and specific to medical malpractice, was lost to moderation. Now that the Supreme Court has ruled that the PPACA's individual mandate [requiring certain people to purchase insurance] is constitutional, health care reform on this grand a scale will likely not face further political upheaval for quite some time. This means that further initiative is necessary to address the legal side of medical malpractice. Unfortunately, the current climate in Congress is not conducive to improving upon the PPACA. Democrats have divided over the necessity of the individual mandate. When the PPACA was initially deemed invalid in *Florida v. Department of Health and Human Services*, moderate Democrats proposed alternatives to the individual mandate, while more liberal Democrats held on strong to the "essential" individual mandate element of the PPACA despite its potential unconstitutionality. Meanwhile, the White House has had problems with GOP [Republican] governors who have been slow to implement the PPACA, and critical of its funding and constitutionality. With internal Democratic turmoil, and increasing eagerness to repeal the PPACA within the Republican

Party, it looks like healthcare reform may have hit another stalemate and medical malpractice reform will continue to go unlooked.

Ongoing Crisis

Some believe that medical malpractice reform is an inefficient way to protect patients from negligent care and reduce the cost of health care overall; the fact is that since the 1960s medical malpractice has been "in crisis." Since then, health care has continued to become more and more expensive across the board. Politicians have attempted to step in to find a solution to both medical malpractice litigation and rising health care costs, however all of these solutions have been inadequate. The PPACA proposes more of the same—politicians stepping in with pilot program type ideas for programs that *might* ease the current medical malpractice crisis. The problem with what the PPACA proposes is that it encourages more bureaucracy—which historically resulted in watered down, ineffective medical malpractice reform and health care reform. If history continues to repeat itself, the PPACA committees created by the medical malpractice grants will continue to create programs that provide minor changes to a system that needs a complete overhaul or the programs that effect change will be deemed too complicated or too extreme. Where the PPACA as a whole, as well as the history behind it, is on point to spur change is the sentiment behind it. If patient care and overall health become the primary focus of our government health care system, the hope is, there will be fewer medical mistakes, less litigation, and less expense.

Organizations to Contact

The editors have compiled the following list of organizations concerned with the issues debated in this book. The descriptions are derived from materials provided by the organizations. All have publications or information available for interested readers. The list was compiled on the date of publication of the present volume; names, addresses, phone and fax numbers, and e-mail and Internet addresses may change. Be aware that many organizations take several weeks or longer to respond to inquiries, so allow as much time as possible.

American Association for Justice (AAJ)
777 6th St. NW, Suite 200, Washington, DC   20001
(800) 424-2725
website: www.justice.org

The American Association for Justice (AAJ), formerly the Association of Trial Lawyers of America, is the leading professional organization for lawyers representing plaintiffs in the United States. Its stated mission is to promote a fair and effective justice system and to support the work of attorneys on behalf of those injured by the misconduct or negligence of others. The organization files amicus briefs in courts, lobbies legislative bodies, and engages in other activities to support plaintiffs and their lawyers. It publishes magazines such as *Trial, Class Action Law Reporter,* and *Professional Action Law Reporter*. Its website includes information on many legal issues including medical malpractice.

American Bar Association (ABA)
321 N. Clark St., Chicago, IL   60654-7598
(800) 285-2221
website: www.americanbar.org/aba.html

Comprised of more than four hundred thousand legal professionals, the American Bar Association (ABA) is a voluntary organization that provides law school accreditation, continuing legal education, legal analysis, research, programs to assist lawyers and judges in their work, and initiatives to improve the legal system for the public. The ABA's website hosts a wide variety of blogs, including several that focus on the US Supreme Court. The ABA also publishes the *ABA Journal*, a monthly magazine exploring a broad range of legal issues, and a variety of magazines, scholarly journals, and books. The ABA provides frequent analysis of US Supreme Court decisions and other legal issues.

American Enterprise Institute for Public Policy Research (AEI)

115 17th St. NW, Washington, DC 20036
(202) 862-5800 • fax: (202) 862-7177
website: www.aei.org

The American Enterprise Institute for Public Policy Research (AEI) was founded in 1943 as a private, nonprofit institution to research matters of public policy and to educate the public on government, politics, economics, and social welfare. One of AEI's main activities is to sponsor research and conferences on topical matters. They also have a website that posts a number of publications, including commentaries, op-eds, research papers, and their monthly newsletter, *AEI Newsletter*, as well as videos and transcripts of its conferences, transcripts of government testimony of its scholars, and schedules of upcoming events. AEI has a publishing division, AEI Press, that has issued a range of books.

American Medical Association (AMA)

AMA Plaza, 330 N. Wabash Ave., Chicago, IL 60611-5885
(800) 621-8335
website: www.ama-assn.org/ama

The American Medical Association (AMA) is the largest association of physicians in the United States. Its mission is to promote the science of medicine in the interest of public health. It works to lobby for legislation favorable to public health and raises money for medical education. It publishes the *Journal of the American Medical Association* (JAMA) and numerous other journals. Its website includes information and resources on numerous issues important to the organization.

Cato Institute
1000 Massachusetts Ave. NW, Washington, DC   20001-5403
(202) 842-0200 • fax: (202) 842-3490
website: www.cato.org

Founded in 1977, the Cato Institute is a nonprofit, libertarian think tank that provides research and advocates for public policy proposals that support a limited foreign and domestic agenda. Their main goal is to promote "the promise of political freedom and economic opportunity to those who are still denied it, in our own country and around the world." Cato publishes numerous journals and books, information about which is available on its website. The site also includes a number of articles on the issue of medical malpractice.

Center for American Progress (CAP)
1333 H St. NW, 10th Floor, Washington, DC   20005
(202) 682-1611 • fax: (202) 682-1867
e-mail: progress@americanprogress.org
website: www.americanprogress.org

Founded in 2003, the Center for American Progress (CAP) is a progressive think tank that researches, formulates, and advocates for a bold, progressive public policy agenda. Their aim is to restore America's global leadership; develop clean, alternative energies that support a sustainable environment; create economic growth and economic opportunities for all Americans; and advocate for universal health care. CAP scholars provide analyses of significant legal decisions and issues, as well as a wide range of books on legal, political, and public policy issues. The CAP website posts informational videos and video discussions, information on upcoming events, cartoons, interactive maps and quizzes, commentary on topical issues, and a listing of publications by CAP scholars.

Legal Information Institute (LII)

Cornell Law School, Myron Taylor Hall
Ithaca, NY   14853-4901
(607) 255-1221
e-mail: thomas-bruce@lawschool.cornell.edu
website: www.law.cornell.edu

The Legal Information Institute (LII) is a nonprofit group that believes everyone should be able to read and understand the laws that govern them, without cost. To make this possible, LII publishes law online, creates materials that help people understand law, and explores new materials to make it easier for people to understand law. The group's website includes the text of federal laws, codes, and rules, as well as extensive archives of US Supreme Court decisions, opinions, and dissents. They also maintain a regular blog.

National Institutes of Health (NIH)

9000 Rockville Pike, Bethesda, MD   20892
(301) 496-1776 • fax: (301) 402-0601
e-mail: NIHinfo@od.nih.gov
website: www.nih.gov

The National Institutes of Health (NIH) is a branch of the US Department of Health and Human Services and the country's medical research agency; it is also the largest source for medical funding in the world. It publishes an extensive array of publications for health professionals and consumers, most of which can be found on its website. Its website also includes news releases and other articles.

US Department of Health and Human Services (HHS)

200 Independence Ave. SW, Washington, DC   20201
(202) 691-0257
website: www.hhs.gov

The US Department of Health and Human Services (HHS) is the government agency that concentrates on the public's health and well being. It is the parent agency of other government health organizations, such as the Centers for Disease Control and Prevention (CDC) and the National Institutes of Health (NIH). HHS manages many services dedicated not only to researching new options to combat disease but also to create informative programs for the public. The department's website includes numerous documents relating to medical malpractice and the healthcare industry.

World Health Organization (WHO)
525 23rd St. NW, Washington, DC   20037
(202) 974-3000 • fax: (202) 974-3663
e-mail: info@who.int
website: www.who.int

The World Health Organization (WHO), created in 1948, is an agency of the United Nations focused on creating and ensuring a world where all people can live with high levels of both mental and physical health. WHO publishes the *Bulletin of the World Health Organization*, which is available online, as well as the *Pan American Journal of Public Health*. Its website includes numerous reports and discussions of medical errors and medical standards throughout the world.

Bibliography

Books

Tom Baker *The Medical Malpractice Myth.* Chicago: University of Chicago Press, 2007.

Harvey Bigelsen, John Parks Trowbridge, and Lisa Haller *Doctors Are More Harmful than Germs: How Surgery Can Be Hazardous to Your Health—And What to Do About It.* Berkeley, CA: North Atlantic Books, 2011.

Marcia Mobilia Boumil and Paul Hattis *Medical Liability in a Nutshell,* 3rd ed. St. Paul, MN: Thomson Reuters, 2011.

Elizabeth H. Bradley, Lauren A. Taylor, and Harvey V. Fineberg *The American Health Care Paradox: Why Spending More Is Getting Us Less.* New York: Perseus Book Group, 2013.

Irene R. Brenner *How to Survive a Medical Malpractice Lawsuit: The Physician's Roadmap to Success.* Hoboken, NJ: Wiley-Blackwell, 2010.

Tom Emerick and Al Lewis *Cracking Health Costs: How To Cut Your Company's Health Care Costs and Provide Employees Better Care.* Hoboken, NJ: John Wiley & Sons, 2013.

Charles Foster *Medical Law: A Very Short Introduction.* New York: Oxford University Press, 2013.

Mark A. Hall, Ira M. Ellman, and David Orentlicher — *Health Care Law and Ethics in a Nutshell*, 3rd ed. St. Paul, MN: Thomson Reuters, 2011.

Lawrence R. Jacobs and Theda Skocpol — *Health Care Reform and American Politics: What Everyone Needs to Know*, rev. ed. New York: Oxford University Press, 2012.

Jerome P. Kassirer — *On the Take: How Medicine's Complicity with Big Business Can Endanger Your Health*. New York: Oxford University Press, 2005.

Beaufort B. Longest Jr. — *Health Policymaking in the United States*, 5th ed. Chicago: Health Administration Press, 2010.

Marty Makary — *Unaccountable: What Hospitals Won't Tell You and How Transparency Can Revolutionize Health Care*. New York: Bloomsbury Press, 2012.

Danielle Ofri — *What Doctors Feel: How Emotions Affect the Practice of Medicine*. Boston: Beacon Press, 2013.

William M. Sage and Rogan Kersh, eds. — *Medical Malpractice and the US Health Care System*. New York: Cambridge University Press, 2006.

Frank A. Sloan and Lindsey M. Chepke — *Medical Malpractice*. Cambridge, MA: MIT Press, 2010.

Periodicals and Internet Sources

Marshall Allen "How Many Die From Medical Mistakes in US Hospitals?," ProPublica, September 19, 2013. www.propublica.org.

Michelle Andrews "Judge Devises Model for Resolving Medical Malpractice Cases More Quickly," *Washington Post*, November 21, 2011.

David Belk "It Ain't the Lawyers: Medical Malpractice Costs Have Been Dropping," *Huffington Post*, November 1, 2013. www.huffingtonpost.com.

Randall R. Bovbjerg "Clinical Practice Guidelines as 'Safe Harbors' Against Malpractice Claims," *The Health Care Blog*, July 22, 2012. http://thehealthcareblog .com.

Demetrius Cheeks "10 Things You Want to Know About Medical Malpractice," *Forbes*, May 16, 2013.

Economist "Medical Malpractice: Offensive Medicine," September 8, 2010.

Robert Glatter "Medical Malpractice: Broken Beyond Repair?," *Forbes*, February 6, 2013.

Michael Hiltzick "It's Time to Fix California's Outdated Medical Malpractice Law," *Los Angeles Times*, July 9, 2013. http://articles.latimes.com.

Philip Howard	"Growing Bipartisan Support for Health Courts," *Health Affairs Blog*, October 2, 2012. http://healthaffairs .org.
Insurance Journal	"Doctors' Fear of Lawsuits Trumps State Malpractice Tort Reforms," August 7, 2013. www .insurancejournal.com.
Ezra Klein	"The Medical Malpractice Myth," *Slate*, July 11, 2006. www.slate.com.
Ilene MacDonald	"Malpractice Reform Key to Reducing Costs of Defensive Medicine," *FierceHealthcare*, June 14, 2013. www.fiercehealthcare.com.
Maxwell Mehlman and Dale A. Nance	"The Case Against 'Health Courts,'" Social Science Research Network, April 1, 2007. http://ssrn.com.
Kathleen Michon	"Medical Malpractice: Common Errors by Doctors and Hospitals," Nolo.com, n.d.
Sy Mukherjee	"Doctors Who Are Afraid of Lawsuits Are Driving Up US Health Care Spending," Think Progress, August 14, 2013. http://thinkprogress.org.
Darshak Sanghavi	"Do We Have a Winner?," *Slate*, November 9, 2009. www.slate.com.
Joanna C. Schwartz	"Learning from Litigation," *New York Times*, May 16, 2013.

Mike Stobbe   "Medical Malpractice Suits: Only 1 in
                     5 Pay," *Christian Science Monitor*,
                     August 19, 2011.

Shirley Svorny   "Could Mandatory Caps on Medical
                     Malpractice Damages Harm
                     Consumers?," Cato Institute, October
                     20, 2011. www.cato.org.

Russell Turk   "Why We Need Medical Malpractice
                     Reform," *DailyFinance*, September 23,
                     2009. www.dailyfinance.com.

Index